Praise for *Engaging*

I love this book. I have walked thr[ough ...]
a serious prodigal and have spent ye[ars praying for ...]
ing to families with prodigals. Carol has put it all together so
well. Her analysis is insightful, her grasp of reality is true, her
suggestions are so practical. The book is filled with love and truth,
with help and hope and humor, and with the grace that makes
redemption and restoration possible.
> —JUDY DOUGLASS
> Author, speaker Campus Crusade For Christ
> and founder of Prayer for Prodigals

Engaging Today's Prodigal gives needed insight into the heart of
a prodigal child and rest for a worried, weary, and grieving parent's
heart. Carol's story provides encouragement and hope along
with practical suggestions in dealing with difficult prodigal relationships. She also lends poignant suggestions for how the church
can better equip our children to face the world's onslaught on a
young believer's faith, thus preparing them to face the world with
confidence.
> —LIZ COWEN FURMAN
> Speaker, author, artist and mother of three teen boys

Insightful and gentle, *Engaging Today's Prodigal* is written by a
former prodigal for those who love the prodigal in their lives.
Devoted parents frequently carry deep blame for the choices their
grown children make. With grace, Carol Barnier dismantles the
myths surrounding prodigals and why they chose their path. Then
she dishes up an extra-large scoop of hope.
> —PEGGYSUE WELLS
> Author of *What to Do When*
> *You Don't Want to Go to Church*

Engaging Today's Prodigal offers hope and healing for parents doubly
wounded, first by the pain of a child who has walked away from their
love and then by the pain incurred by the condemnation of others
around them. Carol writes in the frank, even humorous, style of a

person who herself hiked the road of the prodigal. She offers practical steps to help parents survive the waiting period and clear guidelines for restoring family relationships after a child returns.

—EMILY PARKE CHASE
Author of *Help! My Family's Messed Up!*

Carol smashes myths about reaching prodigals while building a relationship framework that invites change. The most startling concept in *Engaging Today's Prodigal* is that parents of prodigals are often so focused on the wrong choices their children make that they fail to grasp some powerful, positive choices they can make themselves.

—DAWN WILSON
Founder of Heart Choices Ministries;
President of the Network of Evangelical
Women in Ministry, San Diego chapter

I've met so many heartbroken parents of prodigals who had nowhere to turn. Carol Barnier provides that place. May this book find its way to families who need it, and even reshape communities captive to bad ideas about prodigals and their families to become havens of help instead of harm. This is a road map for parents and churches, and needs to be widely read.

—JOHN STONESTREET
Speaker and author for
Breakpoint and Summit Ministries

In our professional capacity, we speak with hundreds of homeschooling parents every year. Many of these parents watch their children grow up with a vibrant and active faith. We also serve those who have one or more rebellious children and have seen the havoc this can bring to a family. Carol Barnier, once a prodigal herself, provides insight and direction for all parents who may be struggling with the trauma and guilt that comes with having a prodigal in the family. If you have a prodigal in your family or want to be prepared just in case, please read this book.

—J. MICHAEL SMITH and MICHAEL P. DONNELLY
President of HSLDA and HSLDA Staff Attorney

ENGAGING TODAY'S
PRODIGAL

Clear Thinking, New Approaches, and Reasons for Hope

CAROL BARNIER

MOODY PUBLISHERS
CHICAGO

Edited by Pam Pugh
Interior design: Ragont Design
Cover design: Kirk Douponce, DogEared Design, LLC
Cover images: iStock | 1672271 and iStock | 4253221
      Photogaphy by Kirk DouPonce
Author Photo: W. J. Bies

       Library of Congress Cataloging-in-Publication Data
Barnier, Carol
     Engaging today's prodigal : clear thinking, new approaches, and
   reasons for hope / Carol Barnier.
       p. cm.
     ISBN 978-0-8024-0557-9
     1. Parent and teenager—Religious aspects—Christianity.
   2. Parenting—Religious aspects—Christianity. 3. Teenagers—
   Family relationships. 4. Parent and adult child—Religious
   aspects—Christianity. 5. Adult children—Family relationships.
   I. Title.
   BV4529.B375 2012
   248.8'45—dc23

                                                    2011043078

We hope you enjoy this book from Moody Publishers. Our goal is to provide high-quality, thought-provoking books and products that connect truth to your real needs and challenges. For more information on other books and products written and produced from a biblical perspective, go to www.moodypublishers.com or write to:

Moody Publishers
820 N. LaSalle Boulevard
Chicago, IL 60610

3 5 7 9 10 8 6 4

Printed in the United States of America

To my mother and father,
who endured my prodigal years,
and managed to love and even like me anyway.

Contents

Getting Started: Why You Want to Read This Book   11

Part One: Myths Debunked

1. Myth 1: Perfect Parenting Makes for Perfect   19
   Children
2. Myth 2: It's My Fault—It Says So in the Bible   30
3. Myth 3: I Can Rescue Him   35
4. Myth 4: This Child Just Wants to Push My Buttons   40
5. Myth 5: If I Can Say the Perfect Thing, My Child   44
   Will Finally "Get It"!
6. Myth 6: If I Can Let Her Know How Badly She's   49
   Hurting Us, She'll Stop
7. Myth 7: My Mistakes Will Scar Her Forever   54

Part Two: Dos and Don'ts

8. Do Advise, Don't Badger   63
9. Do Focus on Boundaries, Not on Behavior   68
10. Do Create a Connecting Place   74
11. Don't Start a Sentence with "The Bible Says . . ."   78

12. Do Sit Down and Listen   84
13. Don't Miss the Courage in Your Prodigal   89
14. Do Love When Your Prodigal Is Most Unlovable   93
15. Do Create a Support System   97
16. Do Save Something for Your Non-Prodigals   101
17. Do Reach Out to Prodigals Who Aren't Your Own   106
18. Don't Pull Out a List of Expectations   110
     When Your Prodigal Returns
19. Do Not Lose Yourself during This Trial   114

Part Three: Holding Out Hope

20. The Long Walk Home—The Rest of My Story   123
21. God, the Artist   134

Bonus Section

For the Church   141
    Stepping Off That Coattail Faith   141
    Why Do We Believe That?   145
    What a Nice Story   146
    Watch Out for the *Ewww* Effect   148
    A Better Look at Mom and Dad   151
    Whatever Happened to Sin?   154
    Dismantling the Club   157
What Some Other Prodigals Have to Say   164
More Resources   169
Helpful Scripture   171
Acknowledgments   172

Children who make poor life choices have been around since the beginning of time. Since the garden of Eden, folks have stepped away from the plan God created for them and broken the hearts of those who love them.

It's nothing new. It's a very old story.

And yet, for a parent of such a child, it is new. It's fresh. And it's exceedingly painful.

You may have this distressing dynamic happening in your own family. You may also have kept it very quiet because there may be great shame associated with a wayward child. You're concerned others will consider that your parenting has failed. But in fact, it may be that no one in your church even knows about the tensions and difficulties your family is experiencing. One thing is absolutely certain, though—you are not alone. In fact, it is highly likely that many others who are sitting around you every Sunday morning face the same sad realities in their own homes.

Something needs to be done. So many families need ideas on what to do differently. So let's get started. Let's spend some time getting to know the prodigal, understanding their actions, and securing a clearer grasp of just what is motivating their actions.

Getting Started:
Why You Want
to Read This Book

The local police car was trying to catch up with the boy's speeding Triumph Spitfire. Just as they both came close to the family property, the brash young man pushed the button to close the security gate, managing to squeeze through just in time, and then watched with delight as it closed in front of the pursuing police vehicle. Riding on the thrill of adrenaline, the boy ground the car to a halt in front of the house, ran inside, and dashed up to his room. But soon the booming voice of his father called him down. The young man met his dad in the study, where his father's grim stare removed any remaining thrill. "I've just spoken with the officer at the gate," began his dad. "He's on his way up, and if he wants to arrest you, son, I'm going to support him."

That incident comes from the teen years of Franklin Graham, son of evangelist Billy Graham.

* * *

He'd been drinking yet again. And as he'd done before, he stepped behind the wheel of a car, but this time he'd taken along his sixteen-year-old brother. During his drunken excursion through town, he hit a garbage can and dragged it noisily all the way home. His father came upon him, ready to berate him for not only endangering his own life, but having been so irresponsible as to have risked his younger brother as well. But the young man, still feeling the effects of alcohol, decided instead to take his dad on, right here, as he challenged him to "step outside" and face him man-to-man.

That episode comes from the years of a young man known as George W. Bush, 43rd president of the United States.

***

The screaming between the young woman and her mother could probably be heard by anyone passing the parsonage. Her pastor-father never argued when she got like this. But while he was always calm, even in the face of such ugly venomous anti-God attacks, her mother just became unglued, trying in vain to plead and influence. In the end, this daughter—the same daughter who had grown up in the church, memorized lengthy passages of Scripture, been the church pianist, taught Sunday school and vacation Bible school—this same daughter would now leave her Christian college for a state school, join the American Atheists, actively work to disarm other young people of their faith, and live a life free of the rules and constraints of her childhood.

That recap comes from the wayward years of my own life.

***

Who would have guessed that any of these kids would make some of the choices that they did? Certainly not their parents, not when they think back to that sweet-faced child they had raised who was taught to love and fear God. Not when they remember the sometimes funny but oh-so-tender bedtimes they could be seen sitting on the bed. And not when they remember the tears this child shed when they learned of some powerful injustice in the world. Not this child. Who would ever have guessed that these kids would one day reject the faith of their youth, and perhaps even their own families? Who of us would ever expect that they could make such amazingly painful, even wildly self-destructive choices?

The Season of the Prodigal

The pattern of the prodigal has been repeated with predictable regularity for thousands of years. Children are raised in a loving, believing home, and still sometimes choose another path. But the sheer number of kids leaving the faith is at a startling high. Why are they going? Where are they going? What are they thinking? And is there anything parents can do to increase the chances that they'll one day return?

It's not just the volume of prodigals however that brings concern. It's also the unprecedented associated dangers. In the days of the New Testament prodigal, the wayward son's excesses led him to working with pigs, squandering his wealth with "wild living," and going hungry. I suppose he might have been at risk from robbers and thugs wanting to harm him as he wandered through the country. These were real issues that his father most certainly would have worried about.

But the ramifications of a prodigal's choices today are so much more grave, the risks of permanent harm so much more possible. A prodigal in Franklin Graham's day would likely drive a fast car or take up smoking. When elementary teachers were asked to name the top five problems in school, there was a time when they cited talking out of turn, chewing gum, making noise, running in the hallway, and cutting in line. Can you imagine? Today's teachers and parents would be thrilled to exchange these problems with the ones they must contend with.

Concerned parents today, however, must worry about those former issues plus sex that starts at a frighteningly early age, abortions, cuttings and other self-mutilations, the lure of the homosexual lifestyle with its long list of self-risking behaviors, suicide rates three times that of previous generations, meth and other drug use, date rape, school shootings, and all of these at rates and levels that would leave those parents of fifty years ago wide-eyed and breathless.

Not all prodigals delve into such seriously self-destructive activities. But tell that to parents who haven't heard from their child in three months. Tell them not to worry about such things when the phone rings at 4:00 a.m. Even if the reality of a child's walk doesn't include such frightening things, the worry in the parent's mind certainly will. The assault comes from all sides. Once upon a time our efforts to protect our children were supported by most of the social structures around us. Our culture used to aid us in the pursuit of child safety. But now, much of a parent's job is to get a child from infancy to adulthood while protecting them *from* the culture.

How Will This Book Help?

There are many forces trying to influence today's kids, and so many possible directions a child might take, that we have a hard time knowing just what language to adopt. The word *prodigal* is used very broadly in church circles. Some parents will turn to this word too quickly by misapplying it to a child who is simply questioning their authority, going so far as to call an eight-year-old a prodigal because he balks at correction. Others may have two children who have left the faith; one who is wild and reckless, the other who is hardworking and successful. Yet they apply *prodigal* only to the irresponsible child. The second child "is finding himself" or "has wandered, but he'll be all right." Still others only use the word *prodigal* for a child who has completed her rebellious journey away from faith and has since returned to the beliefs she was raised with.

In truth, the word *prodigal* has an almost unrelated meaning: extravagant, lavish, sometimes to the point of reckless, sometimes to the point of generous. The young man in the Bible's Prodigal Son story was lavish in his spending; the father, lavish in his love.

It may surprise you to learn that I'm not too concerned with what you call your child or where she falls on the spectrum of possibilities. I know that if your child is questioning her faith, you have concerns. If she is moving into another worldview that dismisses your faith, you have concerns. If she is leaping into self-destructive behaviors that not only put her faith at risk, but sometimes her life as well, you have concerns.

This book deals with the child who, for whatever reason, has defined his worldview outside of the faith, either in part or in whole. We won't focus on the why, but rather on the *what. What do we do now?* My goal here is to give you as parents tools that will have an impact on your relationship with your prodigal for the good, to free you from unnecessary baggage, and to gain an understanding about what is going on in the mind of this person who is rejecting so much that you hold dear.

You'll notice throughout this book that I frequently refer to the prodigal as a child—not because he or she is younger than eighteen. In fact, the information in this book is most easily applied to a child who is technically an adult and has left your family, either by literally moving out or emotionally withdrawing. But I still find myself coming back to the word *child*, because that is the place they hold in our heart.

So what can this book bring to you? The task seems too large, the threat too overwhelming. Perhaps. But in the end, we're still talking about one child, one life, one heart. You don't have to fix the world. That's a God-size task (relief should be flooding over your soul at this moment). Your only job is to reach out to this one child, to do your best to understand why he is so driven to seemingly launch himself away from the faith you hold so dear, and, finally, to maintain and develop a connection that will perhaps one day be a bridge home.

So how do we understand this child? How do we create, build, and maintain bridges of relationship? What are some specific things you can do that would make a difference? That is what this book is all about. In the chapters that follow, I'll not only share with you my own story, but also what I learned from my experiences that may be useful in improving your interactions with your own prodigal.

We'll discuss the myths you might be buying into that are damaging your ability to truly assess the situation. Then we'll look at a list of dos and don'ts that will serve to encourage a healthy and productive relationship with your child during these difficult times. And finally, I'll share with you some resources and other helps, such as what the church can do.

So put the pressures of the whole world in the background for now, stay focused on just one child—your child—and let's get to work . . . one heart at a time.

Part One
Myths Debunked

Many of today's churched kids fall into the category of people seeking a worldview that demonstrates clarity and truth. But not all kids who leave their faith do so for this reason. Some are angry, and the cause of that anger is often unknown to their parents and perhaps even themselves. Some are pulled away by what the world has to offer—that's a ploy Satan has used successfully since the beginning of time. Some made one mistake in experimenting with harmful behavior and are now in the grip of something that seems beyond their power to escape.

Many paths lead away from God, all with their own twists and nuances. But before we can consider a plan of action in response to these faith crises, let's move some junk off the table. We need to address myths and misunderstandings about prodigals, clearing our line of sight so we can better see what can be done to be a part of healing for our child.

Let's do some mental housecleaning.

Chapter 1

Myth 1 : Perfect Parenting Makes for Perfect Children

Sandra had always known that perfect parenting makes for perfect children. And if you looked at her family, you just might agree. I mean the numbers were hard to dispute. You see Sandra had eleven . . . count them . . . eleven children, all of whom were obedient, quiet, compliant, thoughtful, respectful, and kind. Whatever the formula was, Sandra had it figured out. In fact, she seemed to have it mastered.

Wherever her family went, people were impressed. They looked upon her trailing clan with immense admiration and respect. This appreciation was not lost on Sandra. She knew she had been a good steward of the little lives that God had sent her way. Her sense that parenting was simply a matter of consistently doing the right things led her to think rather poorly of those families whose children were, well . . . shall we say, "less obedient" than hers. Everywhere she turned she found parents who were getting it wrong. And she regularly and happily shared her assessment of their errors, making clear to these other parents that they simply were not applying themselves as they should . . . as she clearly had. She even suggested that perhaps it was an indication of a lacking in their own hearts, an unwillingness perhaps to submit to God's authority correctly that was presenting itself in the misbehaviors and wayward choices of their children.

And God laughed. And sent her number twelve.

Now of course, I knew none of this when she rather sheepishly approached my table at a conference where I was speaking. But soon, she spilled out all the confusion and dismay that accompanied this twelfth family member. "Everything that worked so well with my other children does absolutely nothing with this one!" She was out of ideas and was at my table hoping I had some. We first shared the frustration that can arise when a child doesn't fit the mold or follow the standard expectations. We talked about the challenges involved in helping a child become what God had in mind when He created him in this unique and frankly puzzling way. But eventually, she worked her way onto a topic that clearly had been pressing on her heart. She confessed that she had been guilty of pride in the past and as a result had been too quick to dispense harsh judgment on other parents. Her voice dropped to a whisper. "I owe an apology to so many people. I know that I have hurt others and unfairly put a burden on them."

Where Did This Idea Come From?

Where did the idea that perfect parenting will result in perfect children even come from? How did we ever bring such a presupposition to the table? What was the source? It certainly wasn't from the Bible. Think about it. If it were . . . if perfect parenting could truly be a guarantee of perfect children, then Adam and Eve should have been flawless. In the historical account from the garden of Eden, we should have witnessed a supreme example of perfect children who made no significantly poor decisions. Instead, what we see is that pride, arrogance, a misdirected desire to be like God, and a willingness to rashly act on it were present even in children parented by God alone.

If perfect parenting was a guarantee that perfect children would result, well then *you* have been given the power to remove both the ability God gave them to think for themselves and the pull of sin on individuals in this fallen world. My, don't you feel strong? Yet of course, none of us has such herculean capabilities, even though we might wish for them. God has ordained that His children and our children will have the pleasure and the risk of making their own decisions.

Please don't get me wrong. I'm not negating the value of good parenting. Absolutely, we should still strive to be the best parents that we can be. There is no doubt that we have a powerful influence over our children. Good parenting has an impact, as does poor parenting. But having an *influence* is not the same as having *control*. Our reach only goes so far. Our children may well make choices that affirm our influence and stay in line with the precepts we have taught. For parents of such children, there is a strong temptation to believe that the good parenting actually *caused* this child to turn out well, to take full credit, to believe that an algorithm was used and they had simply plugged in all the right numbers. This child, they reason, had no choice but to turn out well. Their parenting was obviously compelling. We can only hope that God doesn't laugh . . . and send them just one more.

If the Bible doesn't promote the idea that perfect parenting will result in perfect children, then where else might I locate it? As is my custom, when I begin to explore a topic of interest, I go out and buy buckets of books. I knew that in writing this one, I would need to share my personal journey with you, but I also knew that I wanted to share a perspective that went beyond my singular experience. I further wanted to take the temperature of current assumptions and beliefs in contemporary Christian writing about a child who becomes a prodigal. So off to the bookstore I went.

Most of the books I found were interesting and useful in one way or another. But I was reading one book that frankly made me uncomfortable. It would not be an understatement to say that it eventually made me angry.

Let me start by telling you what one would *hope* to find in a book on prodigals. You'd expect that the authors would take some time to demonstrate their credibility. You know? Something like, *We had a prodigal. Here's the process we went through. Here's what we did right. Here's what we did wrong. And here's the happy ending: our prodigal has come home.*

That would have been the perfect scenario. That's what you hope for.

But that's not what I got.

Instead, in the initial sections of this particular book, I found . . .

We've never had a prodigal. We've had lots and lots of teenagers, but they were all WONDERFUL! Their teenage years were, dare we say it, delightful! Not a smidgen of a problem with any of 'em. No one was disrespectful. No one rebelled. Why, even to this day, we're all great friends.

At this point, I was feeling an uneasy sensation I'd yet to name. But I didn't put the book down. Part of me wanted to. Part of me sensed that something unpleasant was yet to unfold. Part of me began to warm up my shredder, just in case.

But . . .

I realized that if they truly never even *had* a prodigal, then they may well know something that I don't, something that I'd like to know, something that I should know.

While I have not yet had a child who left the faith, I certainly have a child who is rebellious. He and I have gone head-to-head pretty much since the womb forward. In fact, I would argue that he even tried to take control in the womb. This boy thrashed and exerted himself in utero more than any of my other children. I'm convinced that the only reason I won that battle was because it was a contained space and, well, I owned the flesh.

Although, come to think of it, he *was* an emergency C-section, so my victory may have to be reevaluated.

Thus, since I have had experience with rebellion, I guess I *would* like to know what these authors did that permitted them to claim that they never had a rebellious or even a disrespectful child (and did it involve medication?). So I kept reading. About halfway through the book, after hearing endlessly of the perpetual joys brought to them by each of their various children, they finally got to it. The reason that anyone else's teens become rebellious or think about leaving the faith or actually leave the faith is—are ya ready for it?—bad parenting. Yep. They unearthed it for us. They then went on to great lengths to make clear how sorry they felt to be sharing this, but they forged on, for our sake. "Sometimes," they condescended, "the truth hurts."

Frankly, we are typically *far* too willing to accept fault.

Okay, I'm still reading, but my shredder's ready-to-rip light is now blinking.

Here we go again. I can accept that people who've never had a rebellious child might know something I don't. And I can accept that it may be my fault. Who am I kidding? I usually run with glee to the idea that everything wrong with my child is my fault. Isn't that what parents are supposed to do? Guiltland is a place where most of us have pitched a tent or two.

Frankly, we are typically *far* too willing to accept fault.

So I proceed, with my guilt comfortably in hand, and read on to find out what these authors will tell me I've done wrong. I am ready to change. I am ready to turn things around. I am ready to absorb the wisdom they are about to graciously place before me. And here's what I got.

Keep the channels of
communication open with your child.

Wow! Amazing. I hadn't thought of that one. Now I can see what a mistake it was when I put deadbolts on all the locks hoping they wouldn't find me.

Don't hold the leash too tightly,
but don't hold it too loosely either.

Oh good. I am sure glad *that's* cleared up.
And my personal favorite . . .

Encourage your child.

This was new, breathtaking, even profound for me. Prior to this, I had just been chaining my children to a wall and spending the day berating them for the *seriously* bad hair day they were having. And now . . . praise God, I don't do that anymore. (cue harp music)
   Big, big sigh.
   The advice shared by these authors left me exasperated. (Bet you couldn't tell.) The examples they used showcased parents whose errors were so off-the-charts bad that it was obvious to anyone with a pulse that they were doing it wrong.
   But what I needed to know—and what you're probably also asking—was:

   What if you *have* encouraged your child?
   What if you and she *have* communicated well and easily
      and freely all her life?

What if you *did* bring him up in the church?
What if you actually *lived* what you preached?
What if you told him and showed him in a thousand ways
    that you loved him more than your own life?

And what if she *still* moved away from you and from your faith? Because that's *exactly* what I did to my parents. And I have to tell you that I would have felt such agony for them, if in their pain and desire to find answers they had picked up that book. The guilt that would have been heaped on their heads with this improper analysis would not only have been unjust, it could have been unbearable.

During my own son's roughest year, I was certain, absolutely certain, that his difficulties had to be my fault. Although I could see no errors large enough in my parenting to be responsible for his level of anger, I was convinced I must have done something dreadfully wrong. It was a massive weight on my heart. Over and over again, it brought me to my knees, crying out to God to please, please reveal my failings, so that I might fix what I've damaged before it was too late.

In the midst of this challenging period, I packed up my car for a twelve-hour road trip to visit my mother, who was then dying of cancer. During this journey, while agonizing over my son, I was also going to help a frail woman make sense of her situation, clean her house, make her coffee, and find her a decent wig. While making this lengthy drive, I had lots of time to think, time I used to pray over and worry over my child. And en route I was blessed to hear a very long portion of a recording of Josh McDowell talking about kids and their parents. Now if you know anything about driving across Pennsylvania, you'll know why I consider this event to be a divine appointment, even a miracle. Typically, when one is traversing this very long state, it is wise to bring CDs and just forget the radio. Why do I say this? Because while you might get a station, you'll only be able to hold it for about eight minutes before it is gone. Then, a-scanning-you-will-go till you find another. Rinse. Repeat. In fact, continue this action ad nauseam for five hours—the typical time required to cross this beautiful state, and you have some idea of the experience.

It had never even occurred to me that my son had the capacity to make a bad choice in opposition to good parenting.

I was pleased to find (and amazingly hold) a station airing a presentation by Josh McDowell that got my attention. He was talking about the role between parenting and the children that result. Not surprisingly, he felt there was a strong ability of parents to influence their children, and affirmed that loving, meaningful relationships are key. No surprises there. But here's the part that was meant for me. He said, however, that even with this clear and strong ability to influence, he has nonetheless seen children who came from absolutely dreadful backgrounds who turned out well. The parents of these kids can lay no claim to the beautiful adults that their children became. Conversely, he went on to say, he's seen some of the worst kids—kids who've made the poorest of choices—sometimes come from families that were good, decent, completely functional, and loving. Freedom to make their own choices is alive and well. I cried nonstop for two hours.

It had never even occurred to me that my son had the capacity to make a bad choice in opposition to good parenting. Up to that point I had believed that good parenting was compelling. If he's chosen poorly, it *must* be due to an error on my part. But here was Josh McDowell saying it wasn't necessarily so. And over time, after searching the Bible, I found example after example that it was not necessarily so. There it was. Freedom of choice. Alive and well, even in my child. Did I make mistakes in parenting my child? Sure. Were these mistakes so grave as to be a valid excuse for some of the poor decisions he was now making? In the end, to my surprise, the answer I came up with was no, I really don't think so.

For me it was a powerful and cathartic moment, incredibly freeing. Over the course of that two-hour cry, I felt myself letting go of pounds of self-blame and layers of guilt. It peeled off of me in sheets. With every mile, I carried less and less pain. And then, finally, when I was able to catch my breath, I released this child to God. And that was when I made a funny discovery. I was releasing him into the arms of One who'd actually had him all along. I only *thought* I was carrying him. So if I paint the picture correctly, while God was cradling my son in His loving arms, I had been reaching up and grabbing hold, hanging on for dear life, believing it was all up to me. Not the prettiest of pictures, I'll admit.

You know how when you feel a twinge in your spine, you throw something out in your back, and you find that there are repercussions all over your body? Suddenly you notice there's a pain in your hip. Next one appears in your shoulder. Your neck begins to ache, and a throb takes up residence in your head. Conversely, when your back returns to its proper alignment, other problems are resolved as well. When the core is "right," things fall into place. That is exactly what happened here. When I stopped claiming the guilt that I hadn't earned, it changed many things for the better.

I was no longer instantly angry at my son for poor choices since I no longer automatically assumed it had anything to do with me. Please know that I was still open to that possibility—that it actually *did* have something to do with me. I didn't lose my ability to introspect rationally. But I didn't automatically go to self-blame as I had in the past. And this allowed me to hear my son first without going into defensive mode. Our conversations were vastly improved.

But the best thing is that when you let go of it being your fault, you also send out a new message to your child. In the past, you've been feeling personally responsible and thus projecting the idea that this is somehow your fault, perhaps even *all* your fault. You *must* have done something wrong or she wouldn't be in this pitiful situation. Right? Her life would clearly be better if you'd just been a better parent. Now here's the thing—if *you* accept fault for her life not going the way she'd like it to, she'll be more than happy to agree with you. Think about it from her perspective. "Hmmm . . . I can either take responsibility for my own actions or . . . I can blame *you*. Okay. I choose you." Who wouldn't? That math is pretty easy.

But when you let go of this sense of false guilt, the jig is up. Things are different. When these kids can sense that this little game of blaming you for their own bad decisions is over, and that from this point forward, what they do is a reflection of *their* decisions, it's life-changing. And eventually, even empowering.

The idea that perfect parenting results in perfect children is a myth that brings either pride or pain to a family dynamic—neither of which is honest or healthy. Not one of us would say we are a part of God's family as a result of perfect parenting on the parts of our own parents. And yet even with the flaws we bring from our childhoods, most of us go on to make some good choices. Isn't that amazing? Neither perfect nor imperfect parenting needs to be compelling in how we turn out.

We need to accept that the influence of parenting is strong, but not compelling, and then move on to a truthful assessment of what is happening with our child. While Adam and Eve have proven that even perfect parenting does not result in flawless children, we also have blessed biblical proof that whenever things go wrong, God, in His mercy, is always ready to create for us a new and beautiful plan.

Reflect: *Have you bought into the "perfect parent" myth? How can you balance your thinking on this point?*

Chapter 2

Myth 2: It's My Fault—
It Says So in the Bible

Oh dear sister so-and-so, we've been praying for that boy of yours. It must be so hard to watch him stray so far. We all just ache for you. We're praying you'll figure out what went wrong, you know, what item you missed in the *train a child up* instructions that caused this sad turn of events."

Have you had *that* conversation yet? Or some version of it? You know, the one that says there's a formula for raising children who stay true to the faith and clearly *you've* missed the boat, to the point where your child may not spend eternity with you in heaven?

Yeah. *That* conversation.

It's one of those times that makes me remember something I've often heard: "The Christian army is the only one that shoots its own wounded."

So what is it that could prompt a caring fellow believer to heap such coals on your head?

Let's move to the Scripture that gave rise to this idea: Proverbs 22:6, which says, "Train a child up in the way he should go: and when he is old, he will not depart from it" (KJV).

If you're like many Christian parents, that verse has been a part of your spiritual reference point for years. You took the instruction seriously and did your best to train these children in the ways of God. You do A and you get B. And yet, something went awry. You thought you fulfilled part A. You took them to Sunday school. You took them to church. You discussed living as God intended around the dinner table. Showed compassion to those around you. Didn't speak one way and live another. You lived a life with Christ at the center of your thoughts and plans. You thought you had covered it well. But something clearly went offtrack in part B.

Have you turned to that verse in recent times, begging with God, pleading with God to fulfill the promise you've been told resides in that verse? How many times did you say, "Lord, I've done what You asked. I trained her up in Your ways, in the way she should go, but she departed from it. What is *that* about? I thought we had a deal here."

And you reflect on the verse again. Okay, the verse says *when he is **old**, he will not depart from it.*

"But Lord," you say, "I'm not sure he'll live that long."

As I write that, I feel the pull of two very different interpretations of that statement. The first is a bit funny because some days you're not so sure you won't kill him yourself. His actions go beyond simply illogical to frustrating to ridiculous to sublimely irrational. And on those days you feel like clobbering him. But the second interpretation—far more serious—is that sometimes the behavior of these kids is so self-destructive and dangerous that you have a very real worry that he simply may not survive this challenging time until he can get his head on straight. Such fears are not unfounded. More than one parent has buried a child whose poor choices brought an end to a too-short life.

So the final conclusion, the only obvious place to go from here, since, of course, God *always* keeps His promises, is that *you* failed. *You* didn't train this child up the way he should go.

You did something wrong.

And when we come to such a conclusion, we now carry the excruciating burden of the possibility that we may not see our child's face in heaven because WE BLEW IT.

Ugh . . . the weight of that verse and the accusations that it carries can almost cripple us.

First, I want to tell you I'm sorry that this verse has been so badly abused, and sometimes used to pound on your already tattered heart as you have grieved and cried and prayed over this child of yours. I suspect the person speaking to you meant well, but a poor understanding of this verse, indeed of Proverbs as a whole, turns this beautiful book into a tool used to beat on grieving parents.

So let's take a deep breath, put guilt on hold for a minute, and look at that verse again.

What do we do with a seeming promise that isn't fulfilled? I posed this to a few knowledgeable people and did some of my own research, and I learned that there is much material available on *how* to read Proverbs. I, like so many others, had believed this verse to be a promise. How, then, are we to read Proverbs?

Proverbs are sayings that in general are true, but are not intended to be promises.

The beautiful verses in Proverbs are directions on how we should live our lives. They incorporate into their instruction truths about the nature of God and the nature of mankind. Proverbs are sayings that in general are accurate and full of wisdom, straight from God, but are not intended to be promises or formulas or an invitation to insert a coin into a vending-machine God who will pop out your selection. Think about it. If Proverbs were verses of guaranteed promise, then we have even more issues to deal with.

Do you know any people who have led a life of righteous living and yet have gray hair? (See Proverbs 16:31.)

Do you know anyone who is financially well-off and yet is lazy to the bone? Or how about some really hardworking people, lovely people, who are nonetheless poor? (10:4)

You *shouldn't* know any of these.

In fact, it's downright impossible—that is if all the sayings in Proverbs are to be taken as promises. I don't want you to misunderstand my purpose in this chapter. I believe Scripture is inspired, which means God's stamp of approval is on all of the Canon, including the book of Proverbs. However, as we have seen, there is a difference in proverbs that describe and those that prescribe. You know that a gentle answer doesn't *always* turn away wrath (15:1), but in general, it's better to respond calmly to an angry person. This is an example of a proverb that describes a general truth.

A proverb such as 14:31, "Whoever oppresses the poor shows contempt for their Maker, but whoever is kind to the needy honors God," prescribes an absolute. God cares for the needy, and we're to honor Him by doing the same.

So when we hear, "Train up a child in the way he should go: and when he is old, he will not depart from it," we have learned something that is wise, that is useful, that is instructive. This is an example of a descriptive proverb. It is full of God's best for our lives. We should certainly do so to the best of our ability.

But it is not a guarantee, nor was it ever intended to be so, that our child will not "depart from it," leave the faith, or engage in a harmful lifestyle, even temporarily. You've raised this child in the way she should go. You've given her the best you knew how to give. You really *have* done what you were supposed to do. Now . . . be at peace with that. Set down the burden of angst you've been carrying and know that you've fulfilled your duty. You've given her good instruction. You've put into her mind and heart truths that she carries with her. But at this point, for better or worse, it's up to her. Your acts, while good, are not compelling. As always, God asks that we come to Him willingly, not forcibly.

Now it's between her and God.

Reflect: *Are you so paralyzed by regret that you look inwardly too much? What steps can you take to reverse this tendency?*

Chapter 3

Myth 3: I Can Rescue Him

Brooke had enjoyed the growing friendship between her employee Amy and herself. The company they worked for was full of bright, energetic young women, but Brooke was particularly taken with Amy's unassuming style, dry wit, and solid work talent. They connected quickly, efficiently worked together to achieve company performance goals, and made each other laugh on a daily basis.

There was one problem. Amy was anorexic.

This was clear not only in her frail frame, but also in her willingness to accept poor treatment or poor circumstances as "just how it is." Her view of herself and her worth was skewed. Brooke saw so much intrinsic value in her friend that it pained her to watch. Without even realizing it, she took Amy on as a personal mission. Brooke was certain that with her own love of life, zest of living, and clear belief in Amy's value, she could grab hold of her and virtually carry her into a healthier and happier place.

A little at a time, Brooke began to push Amy out of her familiar routine, encouraging her to try new things, attempting to build a base of successful experiences that would cause her to redefine her self-image. Amy clearly began to grow uncomfortable with all the increasing pressures, but Brooke perceived this as a sort of painful birthing process, with a new Amy about to break through. Finally, an idea grabbed Brooke that she was sure would be cathartic. She planned a big trip for the two of them, out of the country to a sunny, exotic location. She would be taking Amy out into the world, literally and figuratively.

What could be better?

That was it for Amy. It crossed some critical line of "too much." As the days ticked down to departure, she plummeted downward into a self-destroying starvation that soon put her in the hospital at a precarious seventy-nine pounds. The jig was up. The rescue had failed. And what was Brooke's response to her friend's sudden health crisis?

Disappointed? Apologetic? Sorrowful? None of the above. To her own surprise, she was angry, and she promptly abandoned the friendship. While Amy's family and others from the office were visiting daily, Brooke wouldn't even set foot in the hospital. What was *that* about? How could she suddenly drop a friend she had held so dear? One she had invested so much in? It would take years for Brooke to get a handle on it. But she eventually realized that she was angry that Amy hadn't allowed her to be The Grand Rescuer. "She shattered my belief that, through the sheer force of my own joy, I could rescue her. In retrospect, my arrogance was breathtaking." In the dangerous dynamic between Brooke and Amy, it was more than breathtaking—it was almost life-taking.

Brooke hadn't yet learned a basic truth. You cannot save people who don't want to be saved. Actually, the truth is even more basic. You can't save people at all. If they are ready to be saved, they might possibly allow you to be the vehicle. You may even merrily assume that you brought them up and out of their woeful state. It's a rather powerful feeling, but it's deceiving. Make no mistake. If they didn't want to be saved, neither you nor anyone else could have taken them there against their will.

You might have expected that I would have used a story or an example that involved parents and their children instead of two colleagues to make the point. After all, they are the main players in this book's discussion. That would have been a sensible choice. But I found that I couldn't. It wouldn't work. Parents are so blinded by their love of their children, that to tell them at the get-go that they cannot save their child, that they don't have that power, results in a parent looking at me like a deer in the headlights. Lots of eye blinks. It simply doesn't compute. In fact, they're pretty certain that part of their job description *is* to save their child. But we confuse the early concept of *keeping them safe* (clearly our job) with the later goal of them being safe, choosing safe, making safe decisions for themselves. *That* is not within our power. Again I say, we can't save anyone against their will.

The desire to rescue our children runs deep.

And this truth applies to everyone, including our children.

This is usually very hard for a parent to accept. Let's face it. When our kids were younger, we often *could* direct their paths, their choices, even their moods, with the sheer power of our personality, words, or actions. Redirection was easier. Our influence, almost total. But as they grow older, our power decreases as their own increases. Many a parent has watched a child make frightening and self-destructive choices, only to discover that their previous ability to save or redirect this child is no longer operational. Now, when the consequences of their choices are so much more frightening, parents naturally want to plug into that old system and redirect them to a better path. The desire to rescue our children runs deep. The longing to make things right and safe is visceral, instinctive. It's not a head response. It's from someplace in us that doesn't have a name, but where there resides a fear like we've never known.

There comes a point at which parents have to realize that the rules have changed. The power to sway this child's thinking and orchestrate his actions has been vastly diminished or perhaps removed altogether. Continuing to attempt a rescue is energy wasted. Some parents continue with this unproductive and pointless exercise, even though they can see it's not working, because to do less would be to give up on this beloved child. And that's a place they can't go. Guilt and fear keep them coming back and repeating the same useless exercise. But what else can they do? There are better ways to use their energy, and we'll be looking into many of those shortly. In the meantime, it is unproductive and unhealthy for all concerned to continue using a method that no longer works. You may not yet know what you *should* do, but you do have a clear idea now of what you need to stop doing. Let go of the idea that you can save your child. It's not your job. It's theirs. And if you put down that job description, what should you pick up? What do you do now? The rest of this book is full of answers to that very question. You'll come away with many new behaviors to use as a more successful substitute for the ones that haven't been working. I know you still want to do something. You're a parent. You love this child. So let's stop trying to do a job we are unempowered to do, and instead, see if we can find something that has a greater chance at having a successful impact.

Many of us struggle with a desire to rescue others, not just our children. And it comes from a good motive—a desire to be of help. But sometimes we end up more invested in their rescue than they themselves are. We commit our emotions, our sympathy, and our desire for their success in ways that even they themselves do not.

Do you have one of those friends who always seems to be down on his luck, a victim of some unfortunate circumstance, or constantly trying to crawl out of a bad situation? Do you find yourself getting caught up in the excitement of his newest quest for a better direction in his life? Does he frequently call you and want you to invest emotionally (or sometimes financially) in this new idea that will turn things around for him? When his latest plan falls through, do you end up feeling profoundly depressed for him, but then you pause and notice that he himself just sort of shrugs it off and proceeds onward, resigned to a life of renewed misery? What happened here? How could you be more distraught than he was himself?

More is at play in these situations than you can see, factors involved in these people's decisions that are completely off your radar screen.

You're not alone. Lots of people want to help others. But if this situation is the dynamic you've been in, it must change. Even if it is with a prodigal child, you need to let go of the idea that you can be the savior for another adult person. As my first pastor/counselor once told me, "The role of Messiah has already been filled. You need a new job."

Reflect: *Have you been trying to rescue your adult child? How? If so, can you recognize what you may have to stop doing?*

Chapter 4

Myth 4: This Child Just Wants to Push My Buttons

My young daughter was bolting in my direction. I could tell, even from fifteen feet away, that she was very agitated.

"That boy is such a jerk. We were playing chess and he was making up rules and telling me I was wrong and saying all kinds of stupid things. He didn't know ANY of the rules of chess. He just acted like he did. It made me so mad!"

She was a whirling swirling cloud of angry. And while her frustration was reasonable, her level of anger was not. I knew she could stew (and spew) for a very long time if I didn't help her calm down and find her center again. So, summoning my small reserve of Yodalike wisdom, the first thing I did was say that I had something very powerful to tell her. That got her attention, and she at least hit the pause button on her download long enough to hear my almost-whispering voice.

"Think about when you go fishing. While you're on top of the water watching the bobber, let me tell you what's going on down below."

I went on to explain that the fish see the bait slowing sinking downward through the water. They edge closer to check it out. The smell from the bait begins to waft over them. It draws them, pulls them, closer and closer. Eventually, instinct just kicks in. The smell. The hunger. Their nerves heighten. A little twitch of the bait and suddenly, the fish *has* to hit on it. *Boom*. It's done. There's not a lot of thought there. They are hungry. The bait is there. They hit. They don't really even have a choice.

We, on the other hand, have a power that the fish does not.

"When that little boy said that you didn't know how to play chess, it was like he was throwing a piece of bait out there," I told her. "You know full and well that you can play chess. You've had lessons. You've studied. You've competed and sometimes even won. Just because he said it, didn't make it true. What he was doing was just throwing a piece of bait at you, pretty cheap bait at that. And just like a fisherman watching the bobber, he was watching and really hoping you'd hit on it."

She had calmed a bit and was actually listening, so I continued. "But here's the part that gives you power. You . . . are not a fish."

She was watching.

"You have a power that the fish does not."

I could see from her face, this was starting to click.

"You can recognize that goofy comment for the bait that it is. You can see that little boy throw that bait out there, you can watch it land in the water, you can even see him waiting, hoping you'll hit on it. And then here's the cool part—you can just let it float on by."

Her agitation was falling off in sheets.

"You don't have to hit on it, because *you* . . . are *not* a fish."

She got it. This changed things for her. This was a powerful word picture that she called on over and over again when she felt the urge to hit on the baited words of another. It helped her to take charge of her response and maintain personal control. Turns out, I needed the lesson as much as she did. Maybe you've been there too.

You start a conversation with your child over something perfectly innocent, and—*boom*—it happens again. The exchange quickly disintegrates into angry words, bitter pronouncements, and many things you later wish had been left unsaid. The volume escalates. Sentences are interrupted and stepped on. Eventually, no one is speaking with each other—more like at each other. You just don't know how to talk to this child anymore. He knows precisely what to say to zero in on your reaction zones. He pushes every button you have. It really seems almost personal. You sometimes wonder if this whole process is about trying to get a rise out of you just for kicks.

Be cautious about expectations—they can become premeditated resentment.

I don't know about you, but I didn't know I *had* so many buttons until I had kids. If you had told me in my twenties that I would one day be a mom with a temper, I'd have told you that you've got it all wrong. I'm a peacemaker, a Barnabas. I'm a bringer of laughter, a provider of cupcakes, sunshine, and goodwill. My children will never even know what a raised voice sounds like. And yet, buttons just seemed to emerge with the arrival of my children.

I think in the end, the buttons say more about our vulnerabilities and weaknesses than they do about our children. Or perhaps they address our expectations. But we need to be cautious about our expectations—expectations can become premeditated resentment. That's bad enough. But if you have expectations for someone else, if you have a vision for the outcomes in *their* life— particularly a vision that they don't share, it's a guaranteed recipe for conflict.

I'm sure some kids bait their parents almost as sport. But I'm convinced that this is not as common as we often think. I don't believe most kids are trying to push their parents' buttons. The vast majority of the time I suspect it's not even personal. It certainly wasn't for me when I did it, and I know it wasn't for many, many other prodigals.

While I was certainly hurting my parents, it wasn't part of my driving force. I wasn't aiming to hurt them. In fact, truth be told, they weren't much a part of the equation at all. I was *self*-propelled, *self*-motivated, *self*-reflective, and *self*-absorbed. There was a foaming sea of turmoil in my head, and if some of it spilled out on others, I might have felt bad, but I still needed to continue on my journey of self-exploration. I was taking care of myself, and I assume you—the adult in this equation—would do the same for yourself. It might have been unpleasant. But it wasn't personal.

This may or may not be the case with your child. But at least carefully consider this possibility. Because if she is simply attempting to figure things out, your determination to make it all about you will unnecessarily put a wall between you both. Furthermore, if she is really struggling with some issues, you can't help her through it if you keep responding as though this is about you. If you can open yourself to this possibility and see the confusion that is fueling your child's behavior, you may find that rather than feeling angry, you'll feel compassion. You'll sense her personal pain. Your responses will be more tempered, less reactive, and eventually may even be helpful.

Reflect: *Have you felt that your child intentionally tries to reel you in to an argument? How do you generally respond? What strategies can you employ to keep the focus off yourself and on the confusion your child may be feeling?*

Chapter 5

Myth 5: If I Can Say the Perfect Thing, My Child Will Finally "Get It"!

The pitcher steps up to the mound. He contemplates the various factors. How many are on base? What are the strengths and weaknesses of the next up at bat? How crucial are things at this point in the game? He selects a preliminary plan. The catcher makes a hand signal as an inquiry about the upcoming pitch. Fastball? Shake of the head—no. Curveball? Another shake of the head. Slider? Quick nod. Yep. Now the catcher knows what will be coming. The pitcher is pretty much committed to this plan. The greatest likelihood is that he'll go through with it. The catcher could—if he really thought there was a mistake in this plan—call for a little conference and approach the pitcher to discuss options. It's still not too late for some input. But typically he doesn't. And once the ball is thrown, time for input is over. The pitcher, the catcher, everyone can now only watch to see what's going to come of the pitcher's decision.

If you've picked up this book, chances are your child has already decided on a path that concerns you. You may be wishing you had more strongly influenced the decision that led to where he is today. But that ball has already been pitched. Maybe it's a slow pitch and you're now watching the slow drift away, or maybe it's a fastball, sailing wildly forward, unable to be retrieved. Once your child has stepped onto a chosen path, he is likely committed to continue walking it till it reaches its natural end.

In other words, chances are there is little you could say to cause him to step off of it.

Like most parents, you're hopeful you can say that *right thing*, that perfect wording that will resonate with your child and cause him to stop his current direction and step off of this dangerous path. But most of the time, this is a waste of energy, particularly if you're stating views that he's been aware of for years. The window of time during which you might have been able to influence this decision was when he was evaluating potential paths, and *that* happened long before he made the choice you see today. And don't begin the endless "I should have said this," "I could have said that" laments. This is wasted energy. Besides, there's a very real possibility that you said and did all the right things. You may well have given this child the best of foundations, and yet he still chose otherwise. More attempts to influence at this point will be counterproductive. Why?

Here's the tough truth. The ball has to reach its conclusion before the pitcher can evaluate the success of his pitch. In the beginning stages of the throw, the pitcher has every hope that it will hit its intended mark. In the same way, your child's chosen direction has to play out before he'll even be willing to consider the possibility that it might have been a poor choice.

This is a part of human nature. We all want to believe we're sound thinkers who make good choices. We are usually willing to let a decision play out for quite some time, even beyond the point where it is starting to waver, before we're finally ready to admit that our choice may not have been a good one after all. This plays out in the simplest and most innocent of daily decisions. Cooking something from memory rather than following the recipe. Trying to get to a new location without directions. Making a major purchase without investigating reviews. Even with family and friends voicing concerns over our decisions, we usually want to let it ride a bit in the hopes it turns out well and we'll be vindicated. Good or bad, little is lost in such daily affairs. But where you can really see its impact is in highly destructive life choices.

We vacillate from mad to frightened to grief stricken.

When someone we love is involved in substance abuse, self-mutilation, or other alarming behaviors, we often watch her decisions with such pain. Part of the time we're bitterly angry at her negative impact on our lives, and part of the time we anguish over the frightening choices that put her at extraordinary risk, leaving her in danger and leaving us exhausted and emotionally wrung out. We vacillate from mad to frightened to grief stricken. When some new and dreadful event happens in her life, we often think, "Okay, this is it. This time she's hit her low. *This* will be the one that gets her attention and turns her around." But what can often happen is she picks up the pieces and just resumes where she left off. And we're thinking, "Really? Really? *That* wasn't enough to turn her around? *That* wasn't rock bottom?"

Here's the most astounding thing that parents of kids who are now recovered from substance abuse will tell you: The *actual* rock bottom, the actual moment that caused this young adult to turn from his destructive ways and make a true and final move in the right direction often turns out to be a prompt or catalyst that you would never ever have predicted. When the abusers were later asked what was it that caught their attention and got them to begin the process to change their ways, many times the answers seem perplexingly unlikely. The turnaround moments seem almost banal.

- *I saw the face of a happy young boy and I thought, "Why don't I smile like that?"*
- *I couldn't buy a simple hamburger. I didn't have enough money. And I finally said, "What have I come to?"*
- *I saw a young woman on the subway with such perfect and beautiful hair. She moved her head and her hair caught the light and just shone. Mine had been neglected and unwashed for so long that I said, "I used to have hair like that. What has happened to me?"*

With such unpredictable fulcrum points on which major life changes can be leveraged, how in the world could a parent possibly say just the right thing that will be the turning point for this beloved child? The unfortunate answer is we can't. There usually isn't an obvious or clear or sensible "right thing" that becomes the turning point. In fact, sensible seldom enters into it.

So what's a parent to do? Should we make no attempt to reach our child? Should we throw up our hands and just give up? No. Not even close. But it is important to put our energy and efforts into things where we can actually have an impact. This isn't one of those places. Stop searching for those perfect words or that magical key that will unlock your child's ability to see his situation in a crystal clear light. Not only is it a fruitless exercise, it can increase the divide between you and this child.

Try to imagine it from your child's perspective. It seems to him you have only one thing on your mind—finding and using the perfect word or phrase that will wake him up. It reminds me of the old story of Rumplestiltskin. He has a secret name, which once correctly guessed, rids him of the power he has and changes everything. So the sweet young girl he has extorted begins guessing, first through the reasonable choices, and then desperately, through wild and unlikely possibilities. Every time they meet, the more guesses the young girl tries. Next meeting, same thing. She tosses out name after name, one after the other. They can't even have a regular conversation because she must use the precious time she has attempting to determine the mysterious name.

How annoying it must be for our kids when we turn them into a sort of Rumplestiltskin, when we constantly throw possible word combinations at them in the hopes of finding the one that is "right," constantly searching for the magical phrase that completely changes the dynamic, bringing order to the universe. How frustrating it must be for them to never have a regular conversation with us because we are doggedly determined to use each encounter to find and deliver that magical key. There may indeed be a magical key, a phrase that will one day be a catalyst for this child's turn from his current direction. But it is so unpredictable that there is virtually no chance you'll guess it correctly.

Constantly attempting to do so only distances you and your prodigal even further from each other. And in fact, those magical words, when they do come, probably have to come from a source other than you. There are things you *can* do to minimize the damage and length of this child's journey away from faith, but this isn't one of them. Let this one go. Don't continue throwing a barrage of "don't you get it" comments at your child. Let go of making them your daily project. Try to remember how to just talk with your child.

Reflect: *Have you thought that just the right words can turn your child around? Why does this seldom work? How can you let go of making your child your daily project and just talk with him or her?*

Chapter 6

Myth 6: If I Can Let Her Know How Badly She's Hurting Us, She'll Stop

When I first held my newborn son, I was so under the influence of the medication used in the performance of the emergency C-section that I could barely support the 7 pounds 5 ounces of his weight. As I looked into his face, I didn't see anything I recognized. There were no features that I could clearly trace to either side of the family. I didn't think he looked like either his father or me. Clearly still feeling the medication, I handed him back to the nurses telling them that I thought they'd made a mistake and that he belonged to someone else down the hall. (I wish I was making this up.) I'm certain they wondered at the clear lack of bonding they were witnessing. They wanted to see more emotion. I wanted to see more sleep.

In the middle of the night, deep into that sleep, a surgeon came into my room, woke me, and informed me that my child had a life-threatening condition and was being prepped for surgery, even as we spoke. Still in a stupor, I signed the release forms. Then I called my husband, and he joined me at the hospital, where we numbly faced this unexpected and uncertain turn of events. I can't tell you that I had bonded even yet with this child. I was still hovering somewhere between numb, medicated, exhausted, and now . . . fearful.

Eventually our son was taken out of surgery and into the NICU. The nurses got me up on my feet, wound all my various tubes up and onto the little rolling pharmacy pole, and my husband and I began making our way to the neonatal unit down the hall. The surgical incisions made my journey there quite painful, and the lingering medication made my mind still a little fuzzy. I can't tell you that I was yet feeling any meaningful connection to this child.

But then something happened.

I walked into that room full of tiny babies in beeping bassinettes and looked upon my son.

Someone had hurt him.

Someone had cut him open and sewn him shut.

Someone had shoved needles into his tiny, precious, little veins.

And at that moment a powerful switch was thrown. The bond, that only moments ago had seemed vague and whispering, was now screaming in my ears. I truly felt a compulsion to drape myself like a spider over his bassinette and just *dare* anyone to touch him again. I was protective. I was angry. I was now on high alert.

In other words, I became a mom. Even as I write this, twenty-two years later, I begin to cry again, the pain of that moment returning exquisitely afresh. That bond is such an amazing and powerful thing. It pops up seemingly instantly, without warning. You would think something so suddenly constructed would not hold, would be fragile and easily broken. But I've never seen it even waver. It has turned out to be the most powerful, the surest thing I've ever experienced.

We parents know how profoundly we love our children. We can't know otherwise. We feel our vulnerability to this acute love every time we watch them walk out the door. So we also believe that they couldn't actually *want* to hurt us to the extent that they currently are. They couldn't. Not if they truly knew how much we love them. Not if they truly understood the pain we were feeling. Surely they would stop. And I think this belief might be right.

But the problem is twofold.

First, this child, like most young people—but especially young people in personal emotional pain—cannot see or feel beyond themselves. The young adult years are a very self-absorbed time for most of them, even the happy, healthy, and balanced. But for kids in pain, all their energy is focused on surviving and emerging from this emotional chasm in which they now find themselves. This transition period requires an intensity and inward focus that frankly is necessary for the task at hand—figuring out who and what they will become.

Save your strength for battles you can actually win. Having this child fully feel your pain isn't one of them.

Second, and more importantly, even if they were *not* self-absorbed, even if they were basically other-focused, highly caring individuals, I still do not believe that this child or *any* child could ever truly perceive how a parent can love *that* deeply and be hurt *that* painfully by their mere words . . . sometimes it will not happen until they themselves become parents, and even then they just might not grasp the pain they caused.

It's a futile wish. This is just one of those things that is barely understandable or even imaginable without firsthand experience. Our kids are unequipped to comprehend this concept. You would never expect three-year-olds to grasp quantum physics. They simply don't have the needed cerebral hardware to access and comprehend the many complexities. They don't have the prerequisite material. They don't have a child of their own. So we need to accept something. When our child is stepping away from the faith we hold dear, and into a worldview that puts them at spiritual and often physical risk, we will hurt through this process, sometimes profoundly. And it is very likely that this child will not even have a remote possibility of sensing what they've done to us until far, far into the future if they become parents themselves. And sometimes not even then. When she says something dreadful to us and it unleashes this pain of rejection and wounding like no other, there's a very real chance she doesn't know what she's done. She has no sense of its depth. And no explaining or discussion or tears on your part will make her understand it any better. Let it go.

Stop asking questions like "Why are you doing this to us?" "Don't you understand what this is doing to your mother?" "Son, do you know how your destructive ways are killing me?" It takes vast amounts of your energy to attempt to get your child to fully grasp what he is doing to you through this emotional and spiritual battling. Energy wasted. Energy better used elsewhere. Save your strength for battles you can actually win. Having this child fully feel your pain—or the pain of others who care about them—isn't one of them.

I know some of you who are reading this may have a child who knows full well that she is hurting you and actually feeds on it. I don't think they're the norm, but I know they exist. I also know there are kids who know they are hurting their parents, who actually wish not to, and thus eventually steel themselves against caring, becoming almost flippant about the discomfort they create. I still believe both these groups are not aware of the depths of pain they're creating, even if they are more aware than some others. Nonetheless, in the end, your response needs to be the same. You won't get *any* child in the transition process of leaving their faith or their family to feel your pain, not fully, and not enough to change their behavior.

It's worth noting at this point that this very thing—causing emotional pain to a parent without realizing it—is something you and I have done and probably continue to do to our own heavenly Father. How long has He waited for me to understand some concepts? How long did He wait for you to turn to Him? How much more does He wish for us that we don't do because of our human flaws or pride or fear or timidity?

I am convinced that God regularly sends each of us beautiful gifts, blessings He longs for us to open, and yet they sit around fully wrapped, the bows not even tugged upon, because we don't see His love for us. In fact, I suspect the world is littered with His unopened gifts. And His heart, just like our own, must break when His offerings of love to us are missed, or worse yet, dismissed.

So perhaps we can apply grace and patience a bit better with our own children if we pause to remember how much is daily applied to us.

Reflect: *Is it important to you that your child realizes he or she is hurting you? If so, why? Can you let go of this feeling? How can an understanding of grace help?*

Chapter 7

Myth 7: My Mistakes Will Scar Her Forever

This is a hard chapter to write. Much of this book has addressed itself to parents who, while human and imperfect, were nonetheless, basically good parents. These parents haven't done anything so egregious or misguided as to explain a child's walk out of their faith or out of their lives. Such parents often take on unwarranted guilt, dragging down a healthy dynamic with false blame. To them I've offered a type of absolution.

But what if you know you weren't one of those parents? What if your parenting was not the blameless sort? In other words, what if you carry the burden of knowing that you brought something truly destructive into what should have been the safe harbor of your family? The "big" ones, such as alcoholism, abandonment, addictions, infidelity, abuse, whether physical, sexual, or emotional abuse . . . or even some "lesser" evils, but still harmful, such as substitution of authority for a loving relationship, destructive and critical spirit, a poor moral example.

The list of possibilities is a long one, far longer than those mentioned here. The destructive ramifications of actions such as these are well documented. Their reach is deep and typically damages several generations through the common and unfortunate rippling effect. If you were such a parent, there's bad news and good news. And then there's *really* good news. So stick with me to the end.

The Bad News

The bad news is I can't provide a similar absolution for you as I've suggested for others. This isn't something you should dismiss or shrug off. These are serious failings that require a different action. It's possible that your child did indeed leave the faith or the home due to actions on your part or your spouse's part or family patterns. There are situations from which a child was *right* to flee. Even if she did it clumsily and in a flawed manner, getting away from you and your home may be the healthiest thing she ever did.

Unfortunate or wrong past actions on your part and the resulting damage that followed is, to be certain, a difficult burden for you to carry. I imagine that its weight is sometimes overpowering. I do not want to minimize that weight for you, because it is truth, and it is yours to own. So own it you must. But take heart; the story isn't over.

The Good News

Human beings have been flawed—seriously flawed—since the beginning of humanity. Adam and Eve's kids, the first children born of mankind, didn't just flirt with sin. We don't read about them stealing candy from the local market or breaking an earthen pot and lying about it. No, we go straight to murder, and premeditated murder at that. How's that for a leap in severity?

Any one of us is capable of great evil. Nothing could be clearer in the history of man. And yet, the process for restoration has always blessedly been the same.

Admission of sin
Repentance
Restitution
Acceptance of the repercussions of our actions
Acceptance of God's grace

I suspect that if you've made it this far in the book (or by virtue of the fact that you even picked it up at all), it's a pretty good indication that you've already dealt with admitting fault. You're perhaps even past the moment of repentance, having already brought your sins and previous actions before God. This is no small action. I would guess that 100 percent of us struggle to own up to our sins, whether large or small. I've yet to meet anyone who is joyful at admitting fault. But healing is simply not possible until that initial admission is obtained. And yet, it takes a courage that many cannot find. Thus, I commend you for your courage.

I also suspect that, as a believer, you probably went straight from admission to crying out to God for forgiveness. Seeking release from the burden of your sin is a powerful longing. Humbly turning to God is an act of emptying yourself. I commend you for your heart.

So now let's talk about restitution. Longing to make things right is a natural outcome of true repentance. When we really "get it," when we obtain that sight that sees beyond ourselves and for the first time truly observes the impact we've had on others, we long to undo the damage.

You'll note that the above list *isn't* a process for forgiveness; that happens at step two—repentance. God has made this act of eternal import amazingly simple. So you're covered there. Rather, this list is the best sequence of actions for bringing wholeness to those you've damaged. This is about squaring things with others, with those you've hurt. You don't do this to gain God's acceptance, but you certainly will gain His approval. Making things right delights a God who hates evil. You do it out of gratitude for His undeserved goodness to you; you look for a way to pass that goodness along.

I wish I could give you a step-by-step program that provided a clear and guaranteed path to healing. But restitution is going to look different for each situation. And you needn't go it alone. One of the reasons the Christian-based group Celebrate Recovery has met with such success is that there are so many areas of our lives needing healing and so many people seeking help to obtain it. A quick search online will net you many possible resources for finding guidelines for some of the more common behaviors. You'll even find hotlines for groups working with specific issues. Look around. Ask for help. Find out what steps others have taken. Create accountability. Take the first step.

God can even make something beautiful out of those scars.

Here's a word of warning. It's important to know that *restitution does not necessarily mean that you will have a restored relationship with those you've hurt.* In fact, this brings us to step four—one of the hardest of steps—acceptance of the repercussions of your actions. We often mistakenly believe that since we've conquered this issue in our minds and lives, it should now be conquered and removed from the minds and memories of those we've hurt. You know you've done wrong. You're sorry. It's all so clear to you now.

So your children or others should simply forgive you and move on. But the truth is that if you are *truly* sorry for what you've done to them, you will understand that forgiveness—*if* it comes—and restoration—*if* it comes—will be on *their* time schedule. They may need to go through several experiences that lift the pain off of their lives, one layer at a time, before they can even see clearly. They may even need years to create a place for themselves where they feel safe enough to look at the issues your actions brought to their life. It may be decades before they can even consider speaking to you.

They must take the time to heal. You need to own the fact that one of the repercussions of your actions may well be that reconciliation will never come. And while you may long for restoration with this loved one, it is not yours to take. It is only theirs to give. You have one job: do what's right. Then pray and wait.

The Really Good News

Here's the best part. If you're feeling particularly burdened by the destruction you've brought into your child's world and believe the situation to be hopeless, you need to know a powerful truth: Your child's life and outcomes at this point are not dependent on you. What happens from here on out is up to him. He can actually go on to have a wonderful, adequate, even beautiful life, even if it is in spite of you. Yes, he may carry some scars from your impact in earlier years. But this is where God is most amazing. If your child is willing, God can even make something beautiful out of those scars. God is always standing ready to take whatever we have and somehow, in His own mystery, make something glorious. He loves to bless the most wounded with the biggest gifts. People with a passion for a particular ministry most often come with a burden born of a previous experience. It scars them, yes. But it also equips them in ways the unscarred cannot attain.

Ego check: Don't ever get caught up in thinking you've thus done your child a favor by providing these scars that God can now use in miraculous ways. The harm you've done was never

God's wish. Your actions were still wrong. You're fortunate that God's actions are always right. But this last bit of good news should magnify your hope and your prayers for your child. Continue in your belief that her life can be beautiful. Pray that God will bless her with His artistry in her life. Pray that she will be open to His voice and His profound desire to make something good out of her pain. Pray. Pray. Pray.

And you may yet see a miracle.

Your Final Act

You would think that the final step, that of accepting God's grace, would be easy. It seems like that would be something one could relax into like a comfortable chair. But when we see ourselves clearly, when we finally "get it" and have a clear picture of the pain we've caused, very often we can't forgive ourselves. It's easy to enter a state of perpetual punishment, where we daily grieve our poor actions and labor in our grief. We also feel that to become a happy child of God is to be someone who is flippant or dismissive of the pain we caused others. If you've truly communicated your regret and wrongs to those you've hurt, then you actually *need* to demonstrate what the peace of God looks like. It's one of the healing things you can do for your estranged loved one, to show what being reconciled to God can look like.

I'm not saying to have a happy party in their face every time you see them. On the contrary, you still know of your past guilt, and your humble spirit should make clear that you know just how much God had to forgive in you. If your awareness of your impact on others is real, it is unmistakably present. But forgiven you are. Regret and compassion can still go hand in hand nicely with forgiven. None of us, frankly, should ever lose sight of just how much grace God has to apply to our lives for us to reconnect with Him. Humbleness should be our daily garment.

Reflect: *Are there things for which you need to forgive yourself? For which you need to ask forgiveness from your children? Ask God to show you when and how to approach them with these matters.*

Part Two:
Dos and Don'ts

My hope is that you actually feel lighter having read through the section on myths. The weight of burdens on your mind is often virtually palpable, and letting go of incorrect assumptions is amazingly freeing. It changes things. Your mental frame and outlook may be lighter, clearer, possibly even more alert for the first time in years. In fact, you may be feeling an agility of thought that leaves you almost itching for action, ready to do something, something proactive, something different from how you've interacted with your prodigal in the past.

Since the stage has indeed changed, it only follows that what now happens *on* the stage next should also change. So let's walk through some of the things you've maybe done in the past that should be reevaluated. When reflecting on my own experiences, I conclude that there are things that might have made a difference. I've heard this echoed in statements by other prodigals as well. So let's consider some new moves and actions that should perhaps be taken up. And let's see if we can produce, finally, a different result, a different dynamic, a new interaction pattern between you and your prodigal that creates a change for the better.

Do Advise,
Don't Badger

I can't believe you smell of cigarettes again," Dad says, making no attempt to conceal his disgust.

"Really? You can still smell it?" Justin lifts his shirt to his nose to sniff.

"Yeah, me and probably half the folks in church tonight."

"Huh." Justin lets the shirt drop and shrugs. "I'm surprised. I haven't smoked since Thursday. Been trying to quit. Oh well."

"Don't you realize you're polluting your body with poison every time you inhale?" He raises both hands in exasperation and finds himself saying for the 835th time, "Don't you know your body is a temple of the Lord?"

Suddenly Justin's head tilts to the side. His face grows serious. His eyes grow wide as the realization of what his father said sinks in. "You mean . . . I . . . I am a temple? Really?"

The light in the dimly lit kitchen mysteriously begins to brighten. Third Day's "I Will Hold My Head High" begins to cue up on the CD player in the background. Justin's mother enters the doorway and smiles as she sees light dawning in the previously darkened mind of her wayward son.

"Why Dad . . . I *get it* now! I shouldn't smoke! I shouldn't harm my own body . . . my . . . temple. Why I can see it so clearly now. I've . . . been . . . bad."

Justin's face breaks into a holy smile, Mom's face is covered with tears, Third Day begins to really belt it out now, and Dad is on his knees praising God for his son, lost but now found.

This scenario, of course, has never and will never play itself out anywhere but in fiction. And yet there we often are, just like this dad, saying the same thing over and over and over again. Maybe it's the dangers of smoking. Maybe it's drinking and driving. Maybe it's sleeping all day. We can't imagine how this child can possibly miss the truth in what we are saying. It's so obviously true for us that it's almost as if they are arguing that up is down, or the sky isn't blue. And since the truth seems so obviously apparent to us, then in our assessment, it *must* be equally apparent to them. Eventually a new reality sets in. They aren't rejecting what we're saying. They're rejecting us. It starts to become personal.

If we know that saying the same things, even true things, over and over again is never going to produce the desired result, why do we continue to do it? The truth is we have crossed over from advising to badgering. In advising mode, we are sharing a new idea with someone who might find the information helpful. But in badgering, we are simply repeating our views ad nauseum to make sure the listener hasn't forgotten how much we disapprove. Advising is a caring act. Badgering is an assault. We are throwing our repeated words at them yet again because we are annoyed that we have shared our learned and wise thoughts with them and they have simply rejected them, and in essence, us.

Let's see if the point can be made more clearly outside of the parent-child relationship.

Your boss walks into the office. He plops his briefcase, coffee, and bagel on his desk, and soon he heads over to chat about a project your team is working on. As you brief him about the details, he notices the can of diet soda on the back corner of your desk. "I can't believe you drink that stuff. It's not good for you, you know. Have you read the research on long-term exposure to sugar substitutes?"

You nod and endure his brief lecture. "Yeah, I know." But you *also* know that you're going to drink it again tomorrow, and the next day, and probably the day after that.

This might not seem like such an odd exchange. In fact, such interactions happen in the workplace and other venues all over the world every day. But now, imagine that he comes in again tomorrow and says, "Are you still drinking that crud? When are you gonna give it up?"

And then the next day—"Why don't you just pour some poison down your throat while you're at it?"

And the next day. And the next. And the next. And on it goes for months, with no end in sight. After a while you might begin to wonder, *What's up with this guy?* At first it seemed like he was sharing honest and kindly concern. But now, there's clearly more involved here. Somehow, he's become personally invested in the decisions you make in your private choices.

He's crossed over from instructing to badgering.

Change the dance. Bring some calm. Speak the truth.

Sharing a basic truth *is* often sufficient to obtain change in others. Most people want to alter their choices in light of new and true information. But when it is not sufficient, when a truth that should propel a person toward change does nothing, then we must own the fact that something else is at work here. It would be far better to spend our energies trying to find out what that "something else" is than to continually throw a ball against a brick wall.

Your children themselves may not have the slightest clue why they are doing what they are doing. The mix of things constantly rolling through their heads may be almost impossible for them to unravel and make sense of. Repeating instructions over and over is simply adding to the noise.

So what should you do instead?

Change the dance. Bring some calm. Speak the truth. They already know how you feel about smoking or drugs or premarital sex. So acknowledge that. Try instead, "Well, you already know how I feel about such things. I'm sure that repeating it would only annoy you. But I'll always love you. You will always be my son."

Several good things happen with those statements.

1. It takes the pressure off this kid to produce a clear answer for a very unclear behavior. If he doesn't yet know why he's making these self-destructive choices, it will only bring frustration (or lies) when he tries to give you a reason from his confused thinking.

2. It makes clear that there is always a path back home. Even when what he does makes no sense, his dad loves him (gee . . . does that sound familiar?). He can hold firmly to that truth, so that when the day finally comes in which the fruit of his bad decisions becomes apparent, he'll see a way back home.

3. It removes a bad energy from the process. It's possible that in this child's mind, much of his energy has to be spent justifying himself to you. It's almost like an unruly dog that is constantly straining against the leash of its owner. It can only think about the powers holding them back. They haven't even yet begun to think about just what would

happen if they rushed headlong into the places they are trying to go.

This straining against our "leash" comes to define them. It also becomes their excuse for their behaviors. "If my parents would just get off my back . . . " By stopping the badgering, you are now officially "off his back." By releasing the leash, he now realizes that where he finds himself is due to his own decisions. That energy that he's spent battling your words of judgment is now freed up to do something more positive.

It also makes something deliciously clear to him. He is now free to go wherever he wants. Life will now be good, he muses. But of course, the bad things in his life that he's been blaming on your over-direction are somehow still around. Turns out it's *not* because you've been "on his back." If that were true, then life should be so much better now. Yet somehow, life is still difficult. And once he realizes this, he will be better able to start the process of focusing his lenses on the true causes of his life's situation.

Change the dance. Bring calm. Speak the truth.

Reflect: *Do you recognize times you cross from advising to badgering? Are there triggers that push you over the line? How will you change the dance and bring some calm, while still speaking the truth?*

Chapter 9

Do Focus
on Boundaries,
Not on Behavior

Adam had stopped by the house early one Saturday morning to pick up some of his old CDs. He was sitting at the kitchen table, having some coffee next to his eight-year-old brother, who was eating breakfast. He hadn't been by the house in over two months, so the brothers were happy to see each other again and were laughing happily together when Dad came downstairs. Adam and his father shared a guarded hello. Dad walked past the boys to pour his own coffee and then turned back to the pair only to notice the new tattoo emblazoned across his son's neck.

"What have you done now?"

The giggles stopped. The younger boy froze. And the mood immediately changed.

"Whaddya mean?"

"That *thing* on your neck. It's massive." In an exasperated whisper, "For crying out loud, son. I never know what you're going to do next."

"I thought it was wicked awesome."

"How about wicked expensive. How can you possibly have

money for that when you haven't paid off your court fines for your last DUI?"

"I'll work it out, Dad."

The playful mood of just a moment ago is gone. Dad leaves the room in disgust. The younger brother looks deeply into his cereal bowl, uncertain of what to do next. And Adam quietly grabs his CDs and exits the house.

Dad needs to examine that conversation. What, exactly, was gained by this exchange? What was the useful purpose of his questions? Did anyone impart new information? Was Adam actually unaware before this moment of his father's dislike of tattoos? No. So why did Dad voice it? Was Adam truly clueless that his father would disapprove of the frivolous expense? No. So why did Dad feel the need to share his displeasure for perhaps the 3,000th time?

Dad expressed these thoughts because he's understandably frustrated and it makes for a bit of much needed venting. But he does it also because it is habit. He's still operating under the young child/father relationship rules. When a child is young, they need to hear your values expressed. They need to know what things are right, wrong, too much, too little, too near, too far. But after a point, your child knows your values. There's likely nothing about your views on right and wrong that he is not already familiar with. But for reasons that probably aren't yet clear, he simply hasn't adopted them. More repetition of something he already knows isn't going to help, and in fact, most likely will hurt.

"How can hearing me state the wrongness of his actions possibly cause harm?" you might ask. Good question. Imagine this scenario.

You wake up tomorrow and your child says, "Give me a list. Write down absolutely everything that you disapprove of in my behaviors." You accept the challenge, spend a few hours composing a comprehensive list, and then hand it over. Much to your amazement, he goes on to accommodate every single thing on your list.

Everything.

He stops smoking. He attends church. He even sings every hymn and chorus with emotion. He gives up sleeping with his girlfriend. He gets a better job, works solid hours. He cuts his hair. He has that tattoo removed. And you frequently find him chatting with the "silver seniors" at the back of the church.

Everything looks good. By all outward signs, this is a changed young man. Any behavior that was on your list is now altered to line up with the perfect image of a good Christian boy.

But the problem? Your boy still isn't a Christian. He has simply changed his behaviors to accommodate that long list you made. And the question then becomes—just what have you accomplished? At best, you've alleviated some of the consequences of his bad decisions. His body will not be dealing with the assault of smoke. He's not going to participate in an unplanned pregnancy or transmission of an STD. But at worst, he's now going through the motions, farther from the very God you want him to embrace.

He's just playing along.

He has changed his behavior so that you'll leave him alone. In fact, he may even believe that all you *really* care about is not being embarrassed by his actions around other church members. In the end, he may conclude that none of this has anything to do with his heart or his relationship with a Christ who longs for him, both now and in eternity. He's pretty sure it's really about appearances anyway. And if he has bought into *that* lie, then he's now even farther from God. And that is a worse place than when he was simply engaging in poor behaviors.

Far worse.

At least back then, there was a line of integrity between his beliefs and his heart. What he believed, he lived.

In dealing with a prodigal, you need to shift your focus and your conversation away from this child's behaviors. Don't try to navigate his ship in life. Let him be responsible for his own actions. If you stop and think a minute, you already know how to do this. In fact, you do it all the time in your dealings with adults in your world who are *not* your children.

You aren't responsible for others' behavior, but you are responsible for how you let their behavior affect your family.

For example, if you were visiting the home of some friends and discovered that they permitted their children to watch a television show that you believed to be highly inappropriate, you might share your concerns about the show, but would you call up the cable company the next day and cancel this family's subscription?

Not likely.

If you opened the newspaper tomorrow morning and read that someone you work with who lives across town has just been charged with DUI, would you feel compelled to jump in your car, zip over to their house, and take their car keys away?

Probably not.

Healthy boundaries state that because *I* desire the freedom to be permitted to make my own decisions as an adult, I'll give you the same freedom, even when I disagree with the decisions you make. You might share with that TV-watching family once or twice your concerns about the show they're allowing their kids to watch, but to go beyond that is to cross boundary lines. However, if this same family wanted to watch that TV show when visiting in *your* home, exposing *your* children to it, you would be perfectly right to prevent this. You aren't responsible for these parents' behavior, but you are responsible for how you let their behavior affect your family.

When it comes to your adult child's behavior, the same dynamic applies. It's time to focus on boundaries and the impact on *your* life and *your* home, not on his behaviors.

Telling your child not to drink and drive again is an attempt to control behaviors. Don't go there. Instead, ask yourself about how his drinking and driving might affect your family. For example, you would be perfectly correct to tell him he cannot drive his siblings anywhere. That addresses the impact on your family and seeks to establish boundaries. But note—when you share this, be certain that you aren't trying to use it as a weapon in a punitive sense. Your words may be saying, "I'm only limiting impact on the family," but your tone may actually deliver the message "I'm hoping this feels like a punishment because I'm so very disappointed in your choices."

Look at the difference between these two comments.

> #1: Adam, your mom tells me you've gotten yet another DUI. I'm not sure what your problem is, son, but I tell you one thing—you're never taking your brothers anywhere ever again!
>
> #2: Adam, I understand you got another DUI this week. I know that's going to complicate some things for you. I hope you're able to work that out. But in the meantime, please understand that your mom and I just aren't comfortable having you drive your brothers anywhere. We know you love them and want them protected too. At this point, I can't make the decisions to protect you. That's your job now. But I do have to protect the younger ones. We love all of you kids and wish that all this was easier.

In both sets of comments, the boundary being established is the same. But the motivation behind it is clearly different. Keep your actions, your words, and your motives all about boundaries. Let the adult be in charge of his own behavior.

As to the tattoo, his eternal salvation is on the line and you're worried about some ink in his skin? Let it go. In the big picture, it's meaningless. Stay focused on what really matters. And what's that? Three things: It's his heart. It's his heart. It's his heart. All the rest is window dressing.

Reflect: *Restate the difference between boundaries and behavior. Have you tried to force behavior? How has that worked? How can you work on setting boundaries instead?*

Chapter 10

Do Create a
Connecting Place

hildhood is a charmed and charming time.

C Our young kids tend to be interested in pleasing us. They typically want to gain our approval and follow our will. It's part of how they feel secure and define who they are. But as they grow older, they sometimes step away from our will. They define themselves in places other than in our family or our faith. Things have changed. And at this point, we also need to make a change.

Letting go of the desire to control our children is a very hard transition. But we still need to make it. C. S. Lewis believes we have a role model in God's own interactions with us.

> There are two kinds of people: those who say to God, "Thy will be done," and those to whom God says, "All right, then, have it your way."

We need to reach a point where we are able to say to our children, "Have it your way." However, when the truth of that moment arrives, it can be at the end of such a painful and frustrating journey we may actually be tempted to throw up our hands and say,

"Now off with you. I'm done with you till you come to your senses. You are welcome to disappear."

Such a response usually comes after a protracted period of conflict, a long and wearying season that has sapped your willingness for continued interaction. It's a perfectly natural response. But I would caution against going that way and instead encourage the maintenance of a relationship, even if it must be a different one.

Keep in mind, your child is testing out a philosophy. Every theory or philosophy often has, at its heart, a bit of truth. People often leap onto an attractive philosophy because something in it has great appeal, and thus, a bit of fuel. So for a time, they can ride on that piece of truth that fuels it. But unless that ride is fueled by a perpetual source of energy—truth—it will eventually be found wanting and give out due to a lack of sustained momentum. At this point, if the followers are honest, they will need to discard this theory and look for another to replace it.

Let's think ahead to the future a bit. Let's go to what you hope will be the next stage. This philosophy of your child's, once fully explored, eventually loses its appeal. It is spent. It didn't hold the answers she originally thought it would. The shine that was once intriguing is gone. Now what? If she had the slightest inclination to return to you and again explore the faith she left behind, is there any place in your relationship, any portal through which she might comfortably reestablish contact?

If not, it's time to make one.

Try to develop a place where you and your prodigal can calmly, even enjoyably, interact.

Create a Safety Zone

Find an activity that the two of you enjoy sharing. Maybe it's playing tennis. Maybe it's going to bookstores. Maybe it's boating. Maybe it's watching basketball, a movie, a television program. Is there something that once upon a time, long before this crisis in the family emerged, that you and your prodigal enjoyed doing? Is there something your child currently enjoys that you might be able to join her in? Did she develop an interest in history? In attending plays? In home repairs? Find something, anything, you can do with this child.

Try relating to this child as a person who simply interests you.

But take note: just getting together won't work unless you take an extra step. Here's the additional essential component required to make this safety zone work—vigorously defend your time together during this activity against any ugly exchanges. Vow that you will not allow yourself to enter into an argument. Determine ahead of time that you will simply ignore any issue that could invoke an angry response from you. Let it go. Remember, you do not have to take the bait. You are not a fish. Even if your child throws zingers your way in an attempt to pull you into that old, contentious tug-of-war dance you've done in the past, let the bait float by. Keep this zone safe, fun, relaxing, and free of disagreement.

Step Back and See the Whole Person

When you look at your child, if all you can see is the pain of her poor choices, you are missing much of who she is. If, in your eyes, she is defined just as a fallen child, then frankly, it's no wonder she doesn't want to come around anymore. Who wants to be seen only by her mistakes in judgment? Who would seek out your company if she knew that in your mind, she's nothing but a colossal disappointment?

Try to once again see the whole person of your child. Do you remember the other qualities she has? Did she once have a sense of humor? Did she have strong opinions on political issues? Does she have hobbies? Musical tastes? What kinds of TV shows does she like? What does she read? Make a list. Remind yourself of all her other wonderful qualities that used to delight you. Try relating to this child as a person who simply interests you. Find a topic to talk about *other* than the issues on which you disagree. There must be something. Seek them out, develop a conversation, and use these topics to reconnect. The hope is that one day, if she ever comes to the end of her current philosophy or her lifestyle choices and seeks a path back toward the family, she'll know where to start.

Reflect: *What qualities or interests does your child have that you can use as a safety zone for communication? Think of two or three things and plan how you can connect with your child without getting involved in philosophical or lifestyle debates.*

Chapter 11

Don't Start
a Sentence with
"The Bible Says . . ."

During the years when I was pulling away from faith, I would often try to engage my parents in debate over the questions I had rolling through my head. My father was not interested in the process. He believed I would eventually work through these issues and make my way back home. Yes, it was perhaps an unfounded leap of faith, but it did keep us from engaging in a vitriolic war of words.

My mother, however, was horrified. She took up the debate with me as often as I would present it. The conversations often grew loud, heated, angry, and usually pointless. I would throw out a problem or supposed contradiction I had found in their theology, and my mother would eventually answer with a sentence that started with "But the Bible says . . ."

It had been her fallback mechanism throughout her life. All wisdom and truth could be found within the verses she had spent so much time putting to memory. She couldn't even imagine a dynamic in which supplying these verses wouldn't provide a simple solution to the dilemma at hand. *If* I had still believed in the truth of the Bible, then she would have been arguing well.

In fact, many generations of kids who were raised in the faith but who left the church still believed in the validity of the Book itself. It wasn't, for them, unreasonable to share what was written in the Bible. Many who left the church and Christian lifestyle realized that though they had made some choices that were contradictory to the Bible, they nonetheless still believed it was truth. However, that is not the case today.

Biblical literacy is no longer a given in our society, nor is a basic acceptance of Judeo-Christian tenets. People cite supposed inconsistencies in the Bible as their reasons for doubting its truth and eventually feel comfortable setting aside the entire Book. Many young adults in this generation have dismissed Scripture as a creation of semidelusional people who need to believe in something bigger than themselves, usually due to a weakness or sense of personal inadequacy. For many young adults today, the Bible is just one of many interesting ancient texts. After all, more than one spiritual book has been written and revered by various cultures. They can't all claim to hold exclusive truth. And in fact, our society reasons, it may be that no one holy book or religion is true.

So turning to these folks and starting with "The Bible says . . ." is instantly ineffective. They're not at all certain why you're basing your life on ancient words written by mere mortals, but they have decided that they won't be doing the same. And to be fair, it's not a completely illogical move on their part. If I had once been an ardent Communist in Russia who now has wholeheartedly rejected this philosophy *and* the writings of Karl Marx, it would be pointless to tell me I should do something because "in the Communist Manifesto it says . . ." It is irrelevant to me what the Communist Manifesto says because I have examined it, indeed lived it, and found it to be wanting, ineffective, flawed, and just not credible.

I may be willing to look to something else as my theoretical base. I *might* even be open to hearing your thoughts, but if you continually refer back to a document I've already dismissed, you will lose my attention.

Yet you're a believer who wants your child to believe. You might by habit and conviction fall back to this well-worn and once effective phrase: "But it says in the Bible . . ." We typically initiate a habit because it serves some greater good. It accomplishes something we value and hold to be true. But when things change, undoing the value of the habit, we're still usually slow to adjust away from what has been, up till now, a very comfortable shoe. It's worded well by Frank A. Clark, who said, "A habit is something you can do without thinking— which is why most of us have so many of them."

So if we can no longer have an impact on our children by starting a sentence with "The Bible says . . ." then what is a believing parent to do? First of all, relax. Just because your child doesn't use the Bible as his life compass, the truth in its pages is still an unwavering force. The concrete laws of God cannot fail to affect them, whether they recognize the source of that influence or not. The Bible continues to be whole, holy, relevant, true, healing, centering, and valid.

Try not to automatically disagree with every point your child makes.

But at this point, starting your sentences with "The Bible says . . ." is the equivalent of casting your pearls before swine. I don't wish to speak so disparagingly of our prodigal child, having been one myself. But there is a point at which he cannot hear you. He will instantly dismiss the words that you're about to share. It may seem disrespectful, but the truth is, you are also dismissing a belief of his. He has stated a clear value of his own; he is not interested in what the Bible says. And yet, you continue to share it, harp on it, from his point of view. Disrespect goes both ways. But if you set aside biblical quotes in your discussion, what *can* you now say in these debates?

If you wish to discourage your child from the excessive drinking, then sharing the Bible's warning against drunkenness isn't going to cut it. Statistics on drinking-related accidents might be more useful. There are also many documentaries on the impact of alcohol on response times, anger management, even crime on college campuses. I think the most valuable thing in these documentaries is to see what drunkenness *looks* like from a sober perspective. It's enough to embarrass anyone.

When my son was young, I regularly tried to share with him the dangers of some of his more rash actions. He always thought I was simply being an overprotective mom. Quite by accident, we began watching a TV show about various ambulance calls. The many different medical emergencies were recreated by actors so that you were "there" before you then witnessed the medical intervention. He saw small children fall through plate glass windows (just like the ones I'd warned him not to run toward). He saw people fall off ladders, tumble over stairwells, impale themselves with electric drills. After several weeks of shows, I began to notice a change in his reponse to my warnings. It wasn't just Mom who thought these things were dangerous. He had seen with his own eyes the ramifications of such scenarios. Perhaps the lesson in this is that it may be useful to grab an outside source, a disinterested party whose credibility cannot be questioned . . . one who couldn't be accused of just being an overprotective mom.

If you wish to engage in a round of apologetics, you can prepare yourself to discuss intelligently and respectfully. Are you trying to win an argument? Or are you demonstrating valid reasons for belief?

What will most interest your child? Is she doubting the existence of God? You can't tell her what the Bible says. But you *can* approach her with the viewpoint that intelligent design evidence abounds in creation, math, harmony, even the concept of randomness.

Is her bent more philosophical? You can find useful material in the idea that when people claim there are no absolutes, they often say so and then go on to paradoxically claim it to be absolutely true. You can't have it both ways. Either there are no moral absolutes, including the absolute that there are no moral absolutes. Or one must admit that absolutes do indeed exist. And *that* is a starting point for conversations on just what absolutes have support and can be deemed credible.

Is she seeking a rational defense for what constitutes moral behavior? You can even use the very notion of right and wrong, of there existing what I call a "giant should" to human behavior that everyone recognizes and falls back on for guidance. This approach too is fraught with fuel for lively debate.

Any of these approaches might be appropriate for engaging your prodigal in healthy discussion. Be sensitive of how and when and how often, and try not to automatically disagree with every point your child makes. Remember that your goal is that your child will one day accept the God of the Bible and embrace for herself the truth because "the Bible says . . ."

In the meantime, I suspect that the better action is in recognizing that *you* are now the only Bible that your child is reading. You will have to *be* the words of Jesus. Let her see Him in your life, your responses, and your love. Let her feel your peace in the face of her tension. Let her sense your assurance in a world that offers few assurances.

Your prodigal is still reading the Bible . . . reading its presence in your life.

Reflect: *Do you tend to revert to "But the Bible says . . ." rather than address an honest question? Do you feel prepared to defend your beliefs, both the tenets of the faith and the reasons for your moral principles? If not, how might you better prepare? (See the resources section on pages 169–70 for ideas.)*

Chapter 12

Do Sit Down and Listen

Winston Churchill has provided us with some of the most memorable quotes and famous speeches of all time. As prime minister of England, he rallied the embattled island nation to stand strong against the forces of Hitler when so much of Europe had already fallen. The threat of losing the war was real. The nightly bombing raids were horrifying. The people were understandably frightened. England could have gone down in many ways.

Yet the people hung on, in no small part due to the well-chosen and powerfully delivered words of Mr. Churchill. Rather than being reluctant to communicate, he was rousing in his speeches, confrontational in meetings with leadership, and he consistently displayed a clear willingness to speak his mind with frank, biting, and sometimes very funny commentary. No one need ever wonder if Winston had something to say on the subject. And yet, it was this Winston Churchill who also said, "Courage is what it takes to stand up and speak; courage is also what it takes to sit down and listen."

I have heard that some parents are so averse to conflict that they withdraw when faced with a confrontational teen or adult child. Not only do they not take the bait that their children float to reel them into ugly discussions, they are so uncomfortable with such challenges that they actually back away from the bait, redirecting the conversation or stepping away altogether.

A real conversation involves a sincere desire not necessarily to agree, but to at least understand.

But much more common are the parents who find themselves snagged into frequent shouting matches in which the same territory is repeatedly covered. What started out as a normal conversation ends up dissolving into regretful words, angry actions, or bitter tears, each side shouting at or over the other. When the child begins to speak, the parents cut him off mid-sentence, certain that they already know what he was going to say. Then when the parents are ready to make a point, the child cuts them off, equally certain that he knows what's coming. These exchanges are fruitless at best, and wall-building at worst, perhaps requiring many years to disassemble.

KEEP IT L–I–T–E

Instead of continuing this futile ritual, consider changing the dance. Try listening in a whole new way. Try to keep it **LITE**. This method has at its heart the familiar but still valuable objective of *seeking to understand before seeking to be understood.*

I've built the components of this communication method on the acronym L-I-T-E.

L stands for LISTEN, as in listen all the way to the end. Instead of interrupting the moment you have an idea of what your child is saying, be quiet. Listen. Wait until you have a clear sense that he is done, that he has downloaded his entire thought, that the agenda is completely "out there." Don't say a thing, unless perhaps it's a prompt to help him continue and finish the downloading process. Otherwise, silence is your only response.

I stands for INTERPRET, as in to interpret or translate someone else's words. "I" also conveniently stands for "IF," which will be the starting word of your response. You begin with "If I understand correctly . . ." and then you proceed to narrate back to him, in your own words, what you believe to be his position (a handy exercise for almost any person-to-person situation). This is not the time to insert your own thoughts. This is not the time for judgment or commentary. You simply reflect back to him, fairly, what you believe his comments represent. Show him that you get it, that you listened, that you have a good grasp of his position.

T stands for TAG IT, as in put a word on it. You are now going to tag this whole response of his with a word that shows that you not only listened, you also felt some of what they are feeling. "T" also conveniently starts the word *that*, which will now be the first word in your empathy response. If he shared something incorporating a clear emotion, then you will address that emotion in your statement.

> "That must be frustrating."
> "That must be annoying."
> "That must be confusing."

If an emotional element had not been conveyed in what he said, then try:

> "That was clearly well-thought out."
> "That has clearly been weighing on your mind."
> "That is an important topic."

This is not a simple replay of his words, but rather goes a step farther and shows a grasp of the impact of his thoughts, the feelings and passion behind them.

You'll notice that all three of the letters thus far are about listening. At this point, you've not had the opportunity to share your own views. You've worked hard to not only give your child a fair hearing, but to make sure he knows that he's received a fair hearing.

Now we come to the final letter.

E as in **EXPLAIN** your position. We've reached the point where it's your turn. But you need to be certain you have indeed gotten everything from your prodigal that he wants to unload. It's important that he has finished. So you start this section with a question.

"Now that I've really heard your position and think that I understand it well, may I share with you my thoughts on the issues you've raised?" If the answer is no, then he probably has more he needs to say first. Work to help him continue the downloading process until he's gotten it all out.

However, chances are, the answer will be yes. Just about everyone is willing to listen when they believe they've truly been heard. Frankly, that's the case with most of us. None of us wants or likes coming to the table for a conversation only to learn that we've actually been invited to a sermon. If we think no one will give us the time of day, we're likely to return the favor. But a real conversation involves a sincere desire not necessarily to agree, but to at least understand. It's all about truly listening to each other. Respectful reciprocity.

LISTEN—INTERPRET—TAG IT—EXPLAIN

Okay. The rest is up to you. Share what's on your mind. Speak truth with kindness. Watch that you're truly informing, not badgering. Be genuine. Be caring. And bring your heart. If all goes well, he'll bring his too.

Reflect: *Have you tried the LITE touch in a discussion with your child? What was the result?*

Chapter 13

Don't Miss
the Courage
in Your Prodigal

The TV cameras zoomed in on the teenager as she dropped her eyes to the floor.

The young bride from a polygamist sect was gently encouraged by the host of a daytime talk show, but even with the kind words of the interviewer, she still seemed fragile and fearful in her answers. The well-known host told her that we were all so impressed with her courage, moved by her actions. We learned that she had been raised in this isolated community, promised to a man much older, and that when her fears escalated, she fled and left behind all she'd ever known. She stepped out, without having any idea where she'd end up.

Worst of all she was still pretty certain, even now, that she was probably going to hell. Throughout her childhood that's what she'd been assured would be the result if she ever left the community.

No one who heard her story would doubt her courage. She had never known anything else. And yet, she had a nagging notion, a simple inkling that things weren't as they were supposed to be. And armed with nothing more than that, she allowed a relentless voice in her head to convince her that there might be something better. She set out and eventually was free.

When we learn of such young women—and others who act so courageously—we commend them. We respond to their plight. We sympathize with the courage it must have taken to leave all that was familiar and comfortable: family, friends, rituals, sights, sounds, smells. Everything that they've ever known, they've bravely stepped away from to obtain the freedom to marry by choice or make their own choices in other healthy ways. We have no problems admiring them. We have no problems recognizing and applauding boldness when we see someone who steps toward something that we believe to be *more* right and away from something we believe to be *less* right. However, we are less able to see courage in someone stepping away from us or our accepted values. We see error, foolishness, confusion, risk, ego. Courage doesn't even make the list.

But for the person who is leaving all that is familiar, isn't the fear factor about the same?

It probably wouldn't surprise you to hear that for many prodigals, leaving the faith of their childhood was a painful experience. That aspect of the decision is often obvious. But had you considered that it may also have been an act of courage? Set aside, just for a moment, the fact that we prodigals stepped onto the wrong path. Leave that discussion for later. Instead, focus on the fact that we stepped out *at all*. Most of us knew exactly what we were losing in this equation:

- The affirming approval of our parents, maybe our grandparents and other family members, even close friends
- The embrace of a community that had surrounded us all of our lives
- A well-established network of people to call on when we needed something
- The patterns and rituals that had been such a huge part of our lives

Why would we voluntarily give this up? What could compel an action with such loss associated with it? Admittedly some kids are anxious to leave the confines of their family's faith. They more resemble a horse ready to burst through the finally opened gate. But *I* did so reluctantly. I liked church and church life. It had provided a wonderful social life throughout my entire childhood. I respected and loved many of the people inside. I knew when I left that I would lose their friendship while simultaneously gaining their disapproval. The church had been my world. I didn't have a similar ready-made substitute in place when I left it. But my need for a worldview that made sense pushed me forward, even if uncomfortably.

Some courage may have been involved in taking the prodigal to where he or she is today.

If your prodigal is out pursuing a life of wild living without constraint, you may not wish to see any courage in their actions. I'll be the first to admit it; this possibility doesn't always apply. Some kids are delighted to leap into a life with no rules other than today's evaluation litmus test—*does it make me happy?* It isn't about courage, but rather self-absorption. But I think we're far too quick to lay that conclusion on them.

Many kids are stepping away from the faith of their fathers today because they don't have a sense that the faith itself makes sense. It seems indefensible. They weren't given the tools to answer today's questions. Actually, they weren't even told that there would *be* questions. They've often lived in a Christian ghetto or protective compound, having little substantive contact with an unbelieving world. The first time they're faced with a defense-of-the-faith question, they lose their footing. The doubts that follow lead to a painful questioning and distancing of things and people they may hold dear. And when it does, it is worth recognizing the forces that must have been at work to give your child the courage to take this major, even if ill-fated, step.

During my toughest years, I wish someone had said to me, "I don't agree with your choices, but I recognize how difficult it must have been to make them and to leave all that was familiar." Words such as these would have been an acknowledgment of the magnitude of my discomfort, an awareness of the force of the ideas that were propelling me, and perhaps a healing balm. Someone speaking to me in this way also would have made me far more open to hearing their opposing views on the decisions I had made.

Being decisive usually involves change, and change is often uncomfortable, whether it's in the right or the wrong direction. Any time a prodigal feels you have an understanding of her experience, she is far more likely to consider your own background or beliefs. So consider this possibility: some courage may have been involved in taking the prodigal to where she is today.

And if you sense that this might be true, share it. This doesn't mean you agree with them leaving or believe that they made the right decision. But it does let them know that you appreciate how difficult any big change is. You appreciate their courage, even if you believe it took them farther from the truth in the end.

Reflect: *Have you considered that your child's step away from the faith may contain an element of courage? In your situation, would it be appropriate to acknowledge that his or her choices might have been difficult to make? If so, how might this open a door of communication?*

Chapter 14

Do Love
When Your Prodigal
Is Most Unlovable

The people gathered around Jesus to hear His latest teaching. In the crowds stood the heads of the local synagogues, the chief priests, the leaders. They had heard rumors that this Jesus behaved in questionable ways, that He had bad taste in friends and even ate with tax collectors and with women of questionable repute. They drew near and then hushed as Jesus began.

"Suppose a shepherd has a hundred sheep. And a little one wanders off, lost, no longer able to hear his master's voice. What should you do? Verily, I say unto you . . . let it go. Good riddance in fact, because if the little ball of wool didn't appreciate the values of the flock, we're better off without it. It's left the protection of our ways. It's rejected its master. I know it's sad, but better to let one go then to upset the whole herd."

Huh?

Or how about if Jesus had said, "Zacchaeus . . . you come down from that sycamore tree. For I'm going to . . . um . . . well, I'd *like* to come over for tea and tell you all about the good news, but see, you're viewed a bit contemptuously by this crowd, and well, I don't want to alienate them. No, no, no, don't even shake My hand. If I touch you, that would be bad too. It might look like I'm kind of wishy-washy on sin. Just know that while God despises you, He loves you too! Isn't that great? If you ever get your act together, maybe we can catch a movie sometime. I'm off to the temple now to catch the two o'clock prayers. Ciao, Zack."

Double huh?

These altered renditions—"fractured" might be more apt— were actually a better representation of the thoughts of many in the crowd, not those of Jesus. For centuries, Jesus has confounded people with His knack of saying just the opposite of what was expected. (It's one of the things I love most about Him.) The New Testament is full of these amazing, unsettling kinds of statements.

> *The poor are rich.*
> *Love your enemies.*
> *I didn't come to call the righteous.*
> *Blessed are the persecuted.*
> *The tax collectors and prostitutes are getting into heaven ahead of you.* (Matthew 5:3, 44; Mark 2:17; Matthew 5:10; 21:31)

Jesus was right in there, touching the unclean, having meals with outcasts, making friends of prostitutes.

The preciousness of the lost to Jesus was a ribbon of thought that ran through all His teaching. You can feel a longing on His part to not only locate, but to also connect with the wayward heart. When He healed the leper in the first chapter of Mark, He could have done so with just a word. But He chose instead to reach out and physically touch this man, to let him feel flesh on flesh, healthy flesh on wounded flesh, something that had been denied the leper by the culture of the day.

This sense of preciousness that Christ extended over people who were on the cultural fringes was an on-its-head kind of statement if ever there was one. Over and over again Jesus made it abundantly clear—there simply was no one so disenfranchised by society that they would also be lost to Him and His loving interest. And Jesus didn't just talk about loving the marginalized while keeping His distance. He was right in there, touching the unclean, having meals with outcasts, making friends of prostitutes.

There it is, the model of Christ showing us how we are to relate to those who have left the fold, who have lost their way, who make choices counter to what we know to be good and true. Our love for them cannot waver and must be apparent to all who watch, most especially the lost ones themselves.

If we're just talking about a kid who's smoking or drinking or skipping out on church, then continuing to love your child may not be so hard. But it may stretch your loving tolerance skills if instead he's up for armed robbery or is stepping into the gay lifestyle or took the life of an innocent young mom and her kids by driving blindingly drunk. It may be harder to feel and show love for a daughter who's on her third abortion or is continually cutting herself or steals money from your purse to support her meth habit.

No, it's not easy. But I would argue that *that* is exactly when your child most needs to know you love her. When she is at her lowest and worst point, when she is—by all current cultural standards—disposable, her need to know that you still love and value her is at its highest point. If he is in a downward spiral of destructive choices, you can be certain that he is finding little of value in himself. He may have his own tape recorder playing in his head: *You are such a loser. You're never going to change. No one wants to put up with you anymore. There's nothing left of value in your life.* Your voice, to the contrary, may be the only positive ribbon of thought about himself that he hears. Don't plead. Don't cajole. Just let him know, no matter what, you can't stop loving him.

When your prodigal lives in ways that you know are wrong, I'm not saying you should pretend otherwise. Truth is still truth. Right is still right. Wrong is still wrong, and he needs to know that. But let's be honest—haven't you covered that base pretty well already? The bigger question now is, does he know that you love him, even with all his bad choices? Does he believe that there is still something in him worth rescuing and recovering? Does he know that if you came upon him in a compromising situation, even if all your fellow churchgoers were looking on from behind you thinking unkind and contemptuous thoughts, does he know that you would still call him down out of his "sycamore tree," greet him warmly, and go home with him for a meal?

No matter how bad a situation your child may find herself in, the distance between you and her is *still* less than the distance between any one of us and the purity of God. Jesus crossed far more territory to reach you and me than you will ever have to cross to reach out to your child. "Above all, love each other deeply, because love covers a multitude of sins" (1 Peter 4:8).

Reflect: *Is your prodigal in an "unlovely" place? What steps—even small ones—can you take today to tangibly show your child your love for him or her? Find Scripture you can use to pray for him or her; try Psalm 139 for a start.*

Chapter 15

Do Create a Support System

People began coming into the room, not in a rush or with purposefulness, but rather dribbling in, slowly, quietly. They took their seats far from one another, not wanting even the slightest possibility of chitchat with other attendees. A few caught me at the door and actually felt the need to nervously say, "I'm here for a friend, not for myself."

There were no animated conversations in pockets around the room like I usually saw when I came to a group for a speaking engagement, no laughter, no one excitedly sharing interesting details from other workshops they'd just been in. Just serious, isolated quiet. I'd never before spoken to such a subdued group. This was my first time publicly sharing my own experiences and insight from my years as an atheist, and now a believer.

I didn't recognize it immediately, but I eventually came to know the prevailing emotion that was evident that day—shame.

In retrospect, I shouldn't have been surprised. I, myself, had waited years to begin telling my own story for the same reason. I'm not proud of the path I took or the self-destructive decisions that I made. I regret the stress that I brought into my parents' home.

But my reasons for keeping quiet were much more self-serving. I knew that a very real loss of status could result by sharing. It was easier to let people believe that I had always been in the church, and that I had never strayed from God's plan for me. I know how to sound as though I've always belonged. I know the old hymns, even back to the earliest music of the church, for I love it all. I know church culture, what's expected, the unspoken rules, how to talk. If the pastor makes a joke about Total Depravity being mistaken for a headbanger group from the '90s, I get the joke. If he says, "Turn with me to Zechariah," I know where to turn. So for years I let my past stay in the past, never bringing it up and just allowing people to assume the best. It was deception by omission.

But I began feeling God's nudge to share. I hoped I was just hearing Him incorrectly and continued to let it ride. One day, however, I was asked by a kind woman in my church to share my story at an upcoming ladies' brunch. Now God's nudge had a date associated with it. So I said a guarded yes, and that was the beginning of putting it out there—the good, the bad, and the ugly. I knew that I would lose that "perfect Christian" picture that I had tried to paint of myself. But I also realized that I didn't have a right to that picture in the first place. I had stolen it. Pretending it was mine was a version of identity theft.

I also came to realize that I'm not allowed to simply be the recipient of God's amazing grace and then neglect to share it.

So shame aside, I began to share. As a result, I have been blessed to play a small part in a giant exhale from so many heartbroken parents. Previously, they had held their breath every time they entered the church, hoping no one would ask how their son or daughter was doing. And if someone did ask, they knew to mechanically smile, mention something vague, then quickly shift the subject in another direction. But in the sharing of my story, and lining it up with their child's own, they saw similarities that eased at least some of their pain.

Others in your congregation need to know they are not alone.

If a child develops cancer or is in a car accident leaving her seriously injured, you have a support network that steps up, understands, cares, and provides. If your child joins the military and is stationed in a dangerous part of the world or if he was mugged outside of his place of business, people would naturally respond with kindness and concern. Your status on their care-radar would actually be more pronounced. But people with a prodigal don't share, because they fear a very different response. They worry—often with some justification—that they or their child will be judged, lose status, and even lose fellowship.

I submit to you today that you need to go ahead and share anyway. Why? Not because you'll activate that concern network that functions in so many other situations. No. I suspect in some ways your fear may well be realized. You need to share for a totally different reason. Because others in your congregation need to know *they* are not alone. In fact, if the numbers bear out the averages, there are *many* someones in your congregation quietly fearing for a child in spiritual and often physical danger. And they sit in that pew Sunday after Sunday believing absolutely no one else in the building would understand. But you know better, don't you?

Terrie Ensley, clinical director at Cross Connections—a Christian counseling organization in Indiana—has held several support group programs for parents with prodigals. She has seen firsthand the healing that comes from such gatherings. "When people begin to speak honestly about their prodigal children among Christian friends, they will find many others who share similar stories. It is then that Christians can do what they were called to do—love one another, comfort one another, support one another, and pray for one another."

There are many good reasons for starting a support system, for reaching out to others who believe that they're alone in this. But there's another very valuable benefit that you may have missed. This will heal some of the pain in your own soul. When it comes to a prodigal, there is so much that is beyond your control. But here is something proactive, something you can do today, something you can make happen that actually makes things better somewhere. Here. In the lives of you and others near you. No, you may not find the compassion and understanding in the general congregation that I wish were there. Stop looking for it. Let go of the need. But you will find it in each other . . . and in looking into God's Word about His heart for your prodigal. Many Scriptures are suggested in the resources section for your encouragement. Explore these and discover God's encouragement for you and for other parents of prodigals.

If you cannot bring yourself to take the larger step of starting a group, at least seek out one trusted believer and share your situation. You need an ear, the support of prayers, and a nonjudgmental, caring soul to confide in. There's a reason why Jesus sent His disciples out in twos. He knows of our need to share burdens, to walk with company on our journey. And He knows all too well the pain and dangers of traveling alone. Allow the body of Christ, which is to reach out to the world, to also reach out to you.

Reflect: *Why are we often hesitant to share honestly with other Christians? See 2 Corinthians 1:3–7. How can you be a comfort to others? What steps can you take to create a support system?*

Chapter 16

Do Save
Something for
Your Non-Prodigals

I sat in a roomful of parents with special needs kids. The circumstances of our children were all very different; many learning and medical needs were represented. But we were all there for the same reason: How do you make family life work when there are such demands required in the care of this one particular child? I'd felt this press against my desire to mother all my children equally for years. Many were the times I'd found myself pouring hours into getting my son through his paces and barely seeing my other children at all. They would dutifully go about their assigned tasks, completing homework, making their beds, keeping themselves occupied and out of the way, steering clear of the focus and tension going on between my son and me in the next room.

What was God thinking? Why would He put such a time-consuming, labor-absorbing, emotionally intense child in the same family as my other compliant, quiet, and reserved children? It just wasn't fair. So often his siblings were overwhelmed by him, his needs, his intensity, his incessant desire for interaction. How can this be a good thing? And how can I possibly give them equal time when this intense child takes the lion's share of my parenting efforts? Just providing basic care for him would often leave me exhausted.

Does this sound familiar? You may well have a prodigal whose poor choices have created fires that you spend many of your waking hours trying to put out. You may be answering calls from the police station late into the night. You may have had to drive long distances to pick him up from his now wrecked car or unexplained appearance in another state. And no doubt, you've also looked upon the faces of your other children and wondered how they're coping, what is this all doing to them. It's possible that you haven't really connected with them in a long, long time because you are consumed with the prodigal and her fires.

The early years of my son's special needs presented a similar dynamic. I realized that one of my children in particular was going to get lost in our family patterns, since so much seemed to revolve around her brother. She was so compliant. So helpful. The last thing in the world that she wanted to do was to add to my burden. If she had needs, she kept them to herself. I knew that this was full of troubling potential. How long could this continue before she would resent her almost invisible status in the family and find somewhere else to feel cared for? So I made a commitment to her. I would make a date to go out for tea, just the two of us. I put it on the calendar at regular intervals. I made it important. Yes, there were a few times when something got in the way, but not many. We can be excused for the occasional postponement as long as it is clear that in the long run, the commitment will be kept. These tea times became so important to both of us. They became our point of connection.

In the beginning, it would take her a good twenty minutes to really warm up and start talking. She was so unaccustomed to having my full attention and was so expectant of interruptions, that she didn't know how to proceed. But we got past that and eventually found our regular tea chats fulfilling to us both. My hope is that someday she will reflect back on our family times and say, "My parents had a lot on their plate, but they always made time to let each of us know we were important to them."

God is able to make something good come of this situation, and not just for your prodigal.

You know I'm about to tell you that you must make some time for your nondemanding child. But first, let me make clear to you—you don't have to give yourself in equal amounts to your children. You can let that one go. However, you *do* have to make some time for those other kids. But set aside your equal-amounts notion, and let's make this work. Your time with this child doesn't have to be days at the beach or a trip on the road. It can be as simple as going out for a cup of coffee, taking a walk on the nearby trail, taking her with you on an errand. But here's the essential ingredient. You must create a moment where you make eye contact, maybe even physical contact, and give her your undivided attention. You must create a situation where she is comfortable sharing what's going on in her head. You can't tell her to follow you around the house while you distribute the clean laundry and then call that "quality time." Eye contact. Focused attention. A time for no one else but her. Even in small amounts, this regular contact speaks volumes of love to a child. Make it important. Make it happen.

There's also a bit of good news here. I believe that God is able to make something good come of this situation, and not just for your prodigal. For a time I was really angry at God for the mix of needs that presented in my family. It seemed so unfair that these other calm and compliant children were being neglected due to the time-consuming needs of their brother. But I knew that his situation called for this amount of attention. So I began to pray and look for God's blessings. It became an act of trust. Could God, who has a plan for each of my children, create something good from something that seemed loaded with challenges? The answer was yes. When I began looking, I found plenty.

- My other children were developing an awareness of reality and others' needs that went beyond their own skin. Early on, they found empathy and compassion. Early on, they discovered ways in which life wasn't fair and that they had actually received more than others. Early on, they found gratitude that their lives were far easier in many ways than was their brother's. God is good.
- One child was able to assist in Sunday school in reining in a child whose behavior was much like her brother's. Her sense of service and even competence grew because of this experience. Yep, God is good again.
- One daughter is incredibly shy, but with this very intense and highly physical brother to deal with, she toughened up and developed skills she might never have found if all her siblings had been calm and amenable. God is still good.
- My children had to learn to entertain themselves. I have discovered over the years that this is a profound gift for them, one often missing in other families. My children do not believe that it is my job to keep life interesting or entertaining. They have learned to do this for themselves. They have learned contentment. God is all about contentment.
- Siblings of a special-needs child are simply not as judgmental when they meet folks who don't fit a preconceived mold. They are more comfortable in a variety of scenarios that leave others feeling awkward. They've had plenty of experi-

ence in reading the faces of those who are taken aback by their sibling. And they've learned to respond in ways that bring ease to uncomfortable situations. What a skill. God is empowering.

• In many families, children have developed an interest in a medical career, counseling position, or other service-based occupation because their hearts have been touched by the unique needs of a much loved but challenging sibling. Some children choose careers that allow them to have an impact on the laws that protect those unable to advocate for themselves. God has plans for all our children.

In the end, I have often turned to that wonderful verse in Romans 8:28 that says, "We know that in all things God works for the good of those who love him, who have been called according to his purpose." I began celebrating the good that has come. He has a plan for each of my children, and some parts of that plan may well require skills that are developed by this family makeup. You can rejoice in the good that will come of the mix and blend in your family. God can bring good not just in spite of the challenges your family presents, but He can actually bring good from them.

Reflect: *Does your prodigal have a sibling or siblings who could use some focused attention from you? What can you do to offer more of your energy to them? What are some positives God can bring from having a challenging child in the family?*

Chapter 17

Do Reach Out
to Prodigals Who
Aren't Your Own

The Big Surprise. That's what I call it now. When I left the faith of my childhood and began a journey into unbelief, I was in for a big surprise. I knew that the people of my faith community would disagree with me. I knew that they would be uncomfortable with my positions. All of that was a given. But what I also *thought* I knew was that they would now make me their "project," feverishly working on me at every encounter out of a concerned desire to keep me from eternal damnation.

But the truth is . . . they couldn't drop me fast enough. These people, whom I'd known for years, some all my life, believed with absolute certainty that I was now on my way to hell, and the big surprise for me was just how easily they let me go.

Now I'm willing to give them lots of grace, for I can see some fairly good reasons for their seeming abandonment. My searching rendered me a tad intense to the point that I know I was at least annoying, possibly even disturbing. Let's be honest; who wouldn't avoid someone like that? They may also have wisely come to the conclusion that it was more productive to stop engaging me and start praying that God would bring someone to my path I might actually be open to. Those would have been worthwhile prayers; the truth is I had written many of these people off. While praying for someone is not abandonment and may indeed be the most powerful action one can take, the problem is that the object of these prayers is often unaware they are being prayed for. From their perspective, it looks the same as abandonment. All that said, I was still surprised that no one found me worth fighting for.

No one, that is, except for Luann.

Where others stepped away from my awkward questions and disagreeable temperament, Luann jumped in. She took me and my questions on with love and grace and patience. She corresponded with me for months, pushing me in my thinking, asking me to defend the new belief statements I was testing. She wrote long pro-tracted letters to me countering my arguments with reasoning of her own. In the end, neither of us convinced the other. But to this day, I view Luann as the face of Jesus to a confused mind during a difficult season. It took a certain kind of thinking and faith to be the right one to reach out to me at this point. Luann certainly qualified in that way. But it took something more—kindness, gen-tleness, respect, concern, lack of condemnation—and Luann poured those qualities into every letter.

When I look back, I don't believe it was necessarily her job to convince me my views were wrong. At that point, I needed to carry my philosophy out to its own empty conclusions before I could really consider otherwise. No, I believe her job was to be the face of Jesus, to show me that I was still valued, that there was a Christian somewhere on the planet who could disagree with me 100 percent and still find me valuable and lovable.

So here's the possibly startling news: You may not be the person to reach out to your prodigal. There may be so much bag-gage between the two of you that he can no longer hear truth from your lips. The most powerful weapon in your arsenal may well be to fast and pray that God will bring someone onto this path, someone with just the right combination of personality, interests, motives, and heart. But . . . while you may not be that person for your prodigal, you *may* be that person for somebody else's prodigal. There may be someone for whom you are tailor-made for a meaningful connection.

Most of the time, our job is simply to be the face of Jesus to a lost world.

Keep your walking-wounded radar up. Let me repeat that: Keep your walking-wounded radar up. Look around you. Listen for the nudge of the Holy Spirit that prompts you to connect with the heart of another. Reach out to those others miss or worse yet, dismiss.

Watch for the kid who makes a beeline out of church as soon as the service ends. Chat up the kid in the airport with the green hair. Connect with the young woman at work who loathes men. Your job quite possibly isn't to win them to Christ. Your job is just to be the face of Christ, right here, right now, in whatever way they can currently process. Sometimes that means just sharing a Coke and talking about work. Sometimes it means chatting about interesting stuff in the news. Sometimes it means asking them their opinion about something for which they have a known skill. But mostly it means that they look at you and know that in the mind of at least one Christian, they weren't worthy of abandonment.

Don't be overwhelmed by this. There are so many hurting souls out there (and even in here—with respect to the church) that you might be saying, "I can't do this! It's too big." You're right. You're not supposed to do it all. The Holy Spirit will not call you to reach all the lost. He knows your limitations.

Besides, you are not tailor-made to reach everyone. You have a unique mixture of qualities, personality elements, interests, and skills that are better suited for some and less suited for others. You can trust the Holy Spirit's nudge. You will get a specific prompt when you've been called up for duty. It may simply be that you took notice of someone you otherwise typically miss. It may be you find yourself on the train with this one, you're stuck in a long line with that one—you have unexpected access to someone whose path rarely crosses your own. It may even be that you feel that familiar sensation of critical judgment and God suddenly prompts you to make a real connection with this individual to find the compassion He wants to grow in *you*. Most of the time, our job is simply to be the face of Jesus to a lost world.

Reflect: *Can you identify someone else's teen or grown child in your church who might benefit from some attention from you? What about someone who has left or all but left the church? How can you take an interest in him or her? Is there someone you will ask to take an interest in your child?*

Chapter 18

Don't Pull Out a List of Expectations When Your Prodigal Returns

There was a day, a single event, when I came to faith. I knew that I had crossed a great divide and become a believer.

You would think that on that day I would have immediately picked up the phone and called my parents. It only makes sense that I would want to share the good news with people so invested in my decision. They had been affected by my atheism and subsequent life choices for many years. They had spent hours praying for me. They had felt the anguished burden of loving a child who may or may not join them in heaven. But I didn't call. In fact, I didn't share my change in faith with them for over a year. What was that about? Why would I be reluctant to share my newfound faith with the very people who cared most about my decision?

It's a little hard to explain. But the short version is that I didn't want to be put into a box of their expectations. When I left the faith, I had made clear my desire to unburden myself of their God. I almost gleefully stepped onto a now-flat playing field. All philosophies and worldviews were now fair game; no particular one rose above the others as an obvious choice of a new belief to embrace. I was open to anything.

But when I had exhausted all these new avenues and was once again ready to believe in the God of the Bible, I needed to proceed very, very slowly. Yes, I had come to a place where I now believed in God, but that didn't mean I was ready to take back the prepackaged God of my parents and put Him in my own basket. In essence, I was back where I had been in high school, kicking the tires of faith, ready to test the premises and claims, and finding out what stood up to scrutiny, what had to be dismissed, and what had to be reshaped to line up with God as I was learning Him to be.

In the end, after lots of reading, thinking, and counseling from a dear pastor, I came to share *some* of the conclusions that had been a part of my parents' beliefs. And some of the conclusions I came to differed. But it was important that they be *my* conclusions. This was going to be my worldview, my beliefs based on my discovery and exploration of Scripture. I couldn't immediately jump back into their faith world because I couldn't take the risk that their expectations would influence me or, worse yet, push me away once again. It was a tenderhearted time, and I needed that time to find out what *I* truly believed. I had a small amount of light. There was much I couldn't see. But to ask me to leap far ahead into an area as yet unilluminated was asking too much.

Let *God* reveal what needs to change.

We don't always give new believers time to walk in the light that they currently have. We often want to leap them forward, to give them a greater understanding, to have them walk in the light that *we* have. In other words, we want them to believe what we believe right *now*. But such forced maturing can be dangerous and push the newly emerging believer away. Instead, it needs to be a time of grace and patience and encouragement. There's a wonderful part of the Carol Everett story that shows this dynamic so beautifully.

Carol Everett began a journey that would open doors for her into the business world, give her many opportunities, and provide her with a fabulous income beyond her previous dreams. Carol began working at an abortion clinic. Over time she rose through the ranks and was eventually managing several clinics. Her business goals worked out, and she did indeed become wealthy. But when she felt a pull away from the industry and sought the counsel of a pastor, she did so in steps. She began moving toward faith. At one point, she turned to this same pastor and proclaimed that while she was no longer personally working in abortion clinics, she still thought that choosing an abortion was an acceptable option. This was a critical moment. Many Christians would have simply jumped in with both feet and said, "Oh no! You must let that go now that you are a Christian. Life is precious. And if you really believe, you'll agree that it's precious too." But to this pastor's credit, he took another path. His response directed Carol to just keep seeking Jesus. Take it a day at a time. Let *God* reveal what needs to be a part of your view and what needs to change.

The pastor trusted that God could direct this woman in His own time. As long as she was actively seeking the truth, he knew she would find it. Carol went on to become a powerful voice for the pro-life movement. Her inside knowledge of the abortion industry has been both revealing and condemning. But had she instead received a criticizing sermon at that pivotal faith moment, that capable and persuasive voice for life—and her faith—might have been lost.

If your child makes sounds that she might be opening her heart to faith again, be careful of your enthusiasm; don't jump on this with expectations. Rejoice with her to the extent that she rejoices. But, let him proceed in his own time, in his own way, to unwrap God's truths for himself. If he asks for guidance, by all means, share it. But otherwise, let him walk in the light that he currently has. Don't present her with a list of hoops she must jump through to prove to you that her faith is genuine.

So when that sweet young couple living together next door makes a step toward faith, don't demand that they instantly live apart. When your cousin asks about God and says he wants what you have, don't press him to clean up his language by tomorrow. Did you achieve all that God has in mind for you the instant you were saved? Have you achieved it yet? The advice to you, to me, to that cousin and that couple is all the same: keep seeking Jesus. Keep seeking Jesus. Allow God to reveal Himself in His own time, His own way. You can trust that God can handle this. He's big enough for the job.

Reflect: *We often put our own expectations on to new believers or newly returned prodigals. What are some of these expectations? Which are reasonable and which can we discard as our own preferences rather than God's principles?*

Chapter 19

Do Not
Lose Yourself
during This Trial

It started off as a typical day in this employment agency where we placed temporary workers in local businesses. One of my fellow employees answered the phone. She rambled through our practiced company greeting, but then there was a pause . . . that became a very long pause. Her face grew pale and I knew something was wrong. All she could manage to get out was a "Yes, but—" before this very angry caller would cut her off.

Most of the time our employee placements went well; the worker did what was asked and the customer was happy. But in this case, the employee had not shown up. And this business owner was more than just a tad upset. He was spewing into the ear of this pleasant young employee some of the ugliest, most vile, and angry words that you can imagine. Way out of line.

All of us around her had grown quiet and were just staring. We wanted to give her some support, but all we could manage were pitiful puppy-dog looks. Again she would try to utter something to change the dynamic, but when it was finally clear that she couldn't, she quickly said, "Just a moment," frantically hit the pause button, and turned to all of us standing around her. While holding the phone suspended in the air, she rapidly poured out to us that this customer was alarmingly angry and that she didn't know what to do.

No one moved.

No one wanted to jump in.

Even the office manager held back.

But I calmly said, "Give me the call."

I punched the button and began to deal with this man's over-the-top anger. I gave him time to verbalize his frustration, listened to him vent for a while, and then slowly began to rein in the conversation. In my responses to him he never heard fear or denial or dismissal . . . or a return of his rage. Nor did he hear submission, or cowering, or defeat. No matter what ugly things he said, I never became frazzled or panicked. He simply heard someone who would hear him out and who planned to make it right. After a time, he was ready to listen to a solution, and we were able to move forward.

I think my status in the company grew a bit that day because everyone sat and watched—I literally had an audience—as I calmed this raging man and brought him back to a realm of reason, back to a place where things were now actionable.

I can't tell you that I've always had such an ability. In fact, I'm rather dramatic in my reactions, sometimes a bit *too* intense, which can often bring anything but calm. However, I did have the ability this time. That's because I had a secret.

First, it's important that you know, I liked working for this company, loved it really, and wanted my bosses to think well of me. But something was different. At this point, this job (actually *any* job for that matter) was no longer my defining purpose. That mind-set was new for me. In the years prior to becoming a mother, my work actually *was* my cause for existence. I was as yuppie a yuppie as you might find. But now I was at a new place in my life. I had one child who had survived a very protracted medical ordeal.

But we were finally through it and I very much wanted another (child that is; not medical ordeal). What defined me at that point in my world was that I hoped to become a new mom again. It was all I wanted.

He couldn't shake my world. I was defined someplace else, out of his reach.

And my secret, when I picked up that phone to talk to this explosively furious man, was that I had just learned I was pregnant. My core was covered.

Now here's the lesson in this story. When it came to all the angry words of that man on the phone . . . *he couldn't touch me.* Nothing he could possibly say would bother me. He wouldn't hear woundedness in my voice, because he didn't have the power to reach any part of me that he could wound. He couldn't shake my world. I was defined someplace else, out of his reach. At that moment, I was defined by that sweet child growing inside me. And *nothing* he could say would change that truth. My core identity was safe.

Finding Your Core

Very often in a book like this, the kind of assurance you typically receive at this point is something like "Rejoice. God will grow you in your patience, endurance, compassion." That's all true. I don't mean to minimize those things. And I suspect that your experiences with your prodigal *have* produced more patience (and impatience) than you knew was even possible.

But while these qualities are lovely and valuable, they are

nonetheless based on your reaction to the input of your prodigal child. It's as though you are standing there with a tennis racket, continually responding to erratic serves from an unpredictable opponent. It's all driven by the server, the child.

But now I think it's time to set the tennis racket down and mentally step off the court. Don't worry. Your prodigal will most likely call you back to the game soon enough. And if you feel so compelled, you can pick up the racket and resume the match. But for this moment, let's take a break. Walk with me off the court and into a nearby wooded path for a moment where we can talk.

One of the most natural things to do when you are a parent is to make *being* a parent your core identity. And if you had talked with me shortly after that jarring conversation with the angry customer so many years ago, I might have burbled happily about motherhood being my core identity. But I have since learned that it is important *not* to have my complete identity wrapped up in motherhood either, for that too will eventually rattle and shake. Having your primary identity as a parent is not a good core selection. And yet, at that time, that was my core's identity. Being a mom used to be my cause for existence—my *raison d'etre.*

But eventually, that too had to be adjusted.

I came to realize by God's design, these kids of mine are creatures who will freely make their own decisions. (Although I've talked to God about that and shared my belief that this *may* have been a mistake and should perhaps be reassessed. I'm always at the ready to be put in control of their life plans should He reconsider.) The truth, although painful, is that these children were never mine in the first place. They are God's. And with the freedom to choose given to them by their Maker, they will make choices that I would not make for them. More distressing, I also learned that they must come to God themselves. I can't bring them. What a painful truth. I can influence them, I can build habits in them, I can mirror my own faith to them, but I cannot bring them.

They will one day leave my home, find their own soul mates, and create a new identity—as it should be. I am hopeful and prayerful that they will develop a spiritual life that forever links them with the Creator of the universe. But one of the hardest lessons I had to learn as a mom was that I can't save them. There are very real limitations as to what I can be and what I can do, even as a mother.

So I moved on to the next spiritual core mutation . . . I would make *being my husband's wife* my core identity.

I worked hard at this. I was dedicated. I was tireless. I was so spiritual.

Sometimes my husband thought I was precious.

And sometimes he did not.

And sometimes he was right.

Through the years, I've tried inserting many different identities into that place I call my core. Yet, one by one, I had to set them aside.

Nothing was safe. If you've never had your life shaken, count your blessings. But for most of us in this world, bad things happen. Jobs are lost. Children are hurt. Spouses die. Spouses leave. Car accidents happen. Families grow apart. People dear to us become estranged.

The one identity that is sound, true, and unshakeable is that *you* are a precious child of God.

How then are we to live? What should be at my core? What would give me strength and direction during the worst of times? Everything I had tried had been shaken away. No one was the pure and safe protector of my heart. Nothing gave stability.

So after I took all those things away, I looked in my heart, I looked at my core, and way off in the back, sitting in the shadows, waiting quietly with a patient smile on His face, sat Jesus, the Author and Perfecter of my faith. He met me right where I was . . . not where I should have been.

And He looked on my weary soul and said, "Now . . . make ME your core, and nothing can touch you."

It was the beginning of spiritual and emotional stability for me. I began working to strengthen Christ's position of being at my core, making Him paramount in all considerations of my life.

If being the parent of your children is your core identity, you're on shaky ground. If every time they stumble, you find yourself questioning your own value, you're on shaky ground. If every time they make a serious mistake, you find yourself sinking into an isolated depression, you're on shaky ground. If *anything* your kids do has to the power to lead you to believe you are worthless, you're on shaky ground. Our kids are not meant to be our center. The one identity that is sound, true, and unshakeable is that *you* are a precious child of God.

This is how to translate this knowledge into the difficult times you may be having with your prodigal. Your life is not summarized completely in being your prodigal's parent. You are many things, many valuable things, things that God put in you because He had a purpose in mind. If you become consumed in your role as parent to a struggling child, you will lose sight of all that you were meant to be. It's okay to have a life. It's not only okay, it's necessary, good, healthy, and desired by your Creator.

You belong to Him. He still has you in His hands. This is the safe core. This is the core that brings peace. This is the core that puts you and your inherent value out of reach of anyone or anything that comes your way. No matter how many balls your child drills down the court in your direction, your core identity should never change. You can return those balls, play hard, invest in the game.

But even if you lose the match, when you walk off the court, you are not defeated. You are not defined by the outcome of that game. You are defined by being one of His own.

It's who you are. You are His.

Reflect: *What are different ways in which we identify ourselves? Our purposes? Do you need to remind yourself that you are a precious child of God above and apart from other identies and what that entails? Here are some Scriptures to get you started: Matthew 5:13–16; John 1:12; John 15:15; Romans 8:28; 1 Corinthians 6:19–20; 2 Corinthians 5:17; Ephesians 1:3–8; Philippians 3:20; Colossians 1:13–14; 2 Timothy 1:7; Hebrews 4:16.*

Part Three:
Holding Out Hope

Thirteen years. That's how long I was an atheist.

That's how long I distanced myself from my parents. That's how long I ridiculed believers and belittled those with a faith with my dismissive shrug. That's how long I decided I could live without a concept of God in my life. I know that compared to some, it's a mere blip of time. But to my parents, it seemed an eternity. They had no indicators they could see in my life that would signify a change of heart was on the horizon. But God of course was ever present on the scene. Seeing all. Watching over. Whispering, *Keep thinking. Keep thinking.* In His wisdom, He would patiently wait for me, knowing that all sincere thinking, all sincere seeking of truth, would always lead to Him. I don't know that in the conclusion of my own story you will see your own child. The details of my story may be quite different from theirs. There are so many walks away from God, so many ways to deceive ourselves. But I do hope you'll find one thing of value that exists in every prodigal's life.

Hope.

Hope that even those most lost to us are never ever lost to the eye of God.

Chapter 20

The Long Walk Home—The Rest of My Story

People I meet today often try to find simple answers for my walk away from faith. In a search to find the formula that might make sense of a child's doubt, they often asked me if there was a single trigger or major issue that led to my questioning. They seem to be hoping for a big and obvious cause.

But I can't satisfy that. I had no overbearing parents, no physical abuse, no oppressing, dictatorial household. Nope. None of these were part of my home experience. My childhood was mostly uneventful and enjoyable. What's more, I would argue that I was blessed with an amazing father. Not only was he a pastor, he was the real deal—a brilliant, funny, caring, and humble man, a combination package that is a rare gift to those fortunate enough to be around such an individual. Everything I heard from the pulpit was exactly what I saw in his life. There were no two sides to this man's walk.

I know that people who have been wounded or disappointed by an earthly father in some way—or whose earthly father fell short in the love department—often struggle to embrace the notion of a heavenly Father who loves them. "God is your Father," they are told, but to them, *father* conjures up less-than-positive impressions.

God's gift of grace and unabashed love doesn't mesh with their set of earthly experiences.

But while I can sympathize and even agonize with them over their obstacles, I can make no claim on such hindrances.

Certainly some events occurred that tore at my faith, but they were found outside of my family. One such obstacle occurred in my youth when a healing service was planned for a much-loved member of our church. This tiny, sweet, middle-aged man named Teddy had the thickest German accent I think I've ever encountered. He was about five feet tall, extremely intelligent, and wore his love for Jesus on his sleeve. Teddy had a faith that blessed and inspired us all. Teddy also had dreadful knees that gave him an awkward, pained gait. And to make matters worse, he was a farmer, so walking about on these compromised knees was not optional.

His condition worsened, and the church decided to conduct a healing service to restore health and mobility to his disintegrating joints. As the time approached, there was a palpable excitement in the air. We were going to see great things of God. We would have the privilege of seeing God's miraculous power on one in our own circle. People quoted Scripture boldly.

- *Ask and you shall receive.*
- *If you have faith as a grain of mustard seed, you can move mountains.*
- *How much more will the Father give good gifts to those who ask?*

I looked forward to seeing all this firsthand. From the way everyone talked, it seemed like a slam dunk. We were coming together to witness a miracle. I was going to be there to see God's power for myself.

You can probably see where this is going.

The special healing service was held.

And Teddy remained the same.

Now this wasn't the problem that tripped up my faith. It was what *followed* the service. When I asked what went wrong, people seemed uncomfortable with the question and the inevitable answer. They commented almost in whispers. The conclusion seemed unavoidable. If faith can move mountains, and then the mountains don't move, the only thing left is to say there wasn't enough faith. Teddy, apparently, wasn't as strong in his faith as we all thought.

Boom. There it was. There was my obstacle.

I had known Teddy for years. His life was such a picture of Jesus applied that I simply didn't buy the lack-of-faith explanation. While others would answer that I couldn't see all the way into his heart, I knew better. I knew Teddy too well to buy this analysis. No one even mentioned the fact that God sometimes just says no. No one said we have no right to turn God into our own vending machine. I now know that this was a misapplication of Scripture. But at the time, it was confusing and even painful for me. Something was wrong here, even if I couldn't articulate it yet.

And a small rip appeared in the fabric of my faith.

I continued to play piano in church, direct the choir, travel and sing with teen performance groups, go to potlucks, read and study my Bible, and teach in VBS. I loved the world that church culture brought to my life. But it didn't keep me from having questions. The commonly asked "problem of evil" question was certainly on my list. How could a loving God permit such evil? But I didn't stop there. Why isn't God an egotist? Who creates creatures, the sole purpose for whom is simply to delight their Creator? And if they don't . . . *Zap!* . . . off to fry city? That takes a pretty hefty ego. And if He can see the future of those who won't choose Him, wouldn't it be kinder of Him not to create them at all than to permit their birth, knowing that they would reject Him and end up in perpetual torment?

Like many young people in the church, I had witnessed some examples of hypocrisy or a clear lack of grace, or met those who used Jesus more as a bludgeon to self-righteously pound on those they deemed lesser in some measure of holiness. It takes a marked degree of maturity *not* to blame Jesus for the mistakes and abuses of His followers. I can't tell you that I had such maturity at the time, but it wasn't the swing vote in my decision to leave the faith. For me at least, the core issue always kept coming back to those questions.

I went off to a Christian college with mixed feelings. At that point, I had enough doubts to leave me only semicommitted about being there. But I *was* looking forward to posing my questions to some PhDs, expecting that they would have the answers to these nagging questions. To my surprise, they didn't have solid responses either. The questions seemed to make them uncomfortable as well —although I will readily admit that my increasingly frustrated tone and deepening cynicism may also have played a part in their discomfort. I was intense. And I wouldn't be at all surprised if that alone wasn't a tad disquieting. Nonetheless, I didn't get good answers.

It's worth noting that this was in the early '80s and the church had not yet developed a strong vision for the value in apologetics that you see today. *Worldview* and *defense of the faith* were not commonly used phrases in church culture at that time. I know that my questions would be better received and handled today in that same college. But at that time, I came away believing that if these learned folks don't have the answers, there clearly aren't any. It's all a ruse, a smoke screen to provide legitimacy for a group of people who have developed a comfortable culture for themselves. It may be a lovely way to live. But it certainly is not a well-developed line of thought that reflects the certainty of God.

I left my Christian college and transferred to a secular state university. You might expect at this point that I plunged into days of wild living, enjoying my lack of constraint. But in truth, my

search actually continued. Just because the religion of my upbringing seemed insubstantial, that didn't mean all faiths were wrong.
I spent perhaps a year researching and exploring other religions.
While this was a fascinating examination that I enjoyed, I eventually would discover some flaw in each group's set of presuppo-
sitions, something that required a suspension of logic and, one by
one, I set them aside. No one, it seemed, had a worldview that
could withstand scrutiny.

My next step was not an uncommon one for those seeking
meaning: I moved on to philosophy. I began studying the views of
well-known philosophers such as Kierkegaard, Nietzsche, Hegel,
and others. I loved the mental playground I had entered. I was
intrigued by the depth of thought and ideas I found. I eventually
chose philosophy as my college minor. I even considered major-
ing in it but could never quite bring myself to take that leap. I
didn't know why at the time, but years later I read a great quote
from G. K. Chesterton that beautifully captured my thoughts.

He said that he too had considered making philosophy a primary area of study, "but somehow, happiness just kept breaking
through." I agreed with that sentiment.

Philosophers seemed, as a group, a fairly dismal bunch, with
far too much self-loathing, or worse yet, everybody-else-loathing,
that didn't sit well with me. And even if they had truth, the misery
that accompanied it wasn't worth the trade-off. But even more
infuriating was that through their playful machinations of thought,
they often wound up in places that were, on their face, clearly
illogical. And rather than admitting that they must have erred
somewhere back in the steps that led them there, they instead
took infantlike delight at presenting a flawed and even vulgar conclusion as fact, even though they could feel themselves that it was
hopelessly disconcerting and at odds with the world as they knew
it to be. It reminds me of another quote, this time by columnist and
commentator George Will, that I've loved for years:

There is nothing so vulgar left in our experience for which we cannot transport some professor from somewhere to justify it.

I had looked at religion and found it wanting. I had examined philosophy and found it useless. It was at this point that I gave up looking and just became an atheist.

As is my habit, I dove into my new beliefs. These were very heady days for me. I felt free and unencumbered in a way that I had never before experienced. I was the captain of my own ship. Life was mine to make of it what I would. I was no longer burdened by archaic modes of conduct or pointless rituals. I had one life to live, and I was enjoying the process of figuring out just how I wanted to live it. I was in charge.

Next, I began challenging young Christians at my university in an attempt to disarm them of their faith. I had the truth, and I wanted to share it. I joined the American Atheists. I ordered pamphlets from their organization to aid me in my faith-breaking efforts. I even attended a meet-and-greet dinner event with Madelyn Murray O'Hair, the woman who brought the legal case before the Supreme Court in 1963 that resulted in government-sponsored Bible reading being prohibited in public schools. She once attempted to leave the United States and become a Soviet citizen, but was turned away at their border. She returned home, founded American Atheists, and began to work toward legal changes in an effort to minimize and eventually remove the influence of religion in American culture. She was the atheist movement's public face, and in many ways, still is, even if posthumously.

This ride was a happy one for quite some time. I did meet with a fair amount of success. I met interesting people. Had fun. Carried no guilt. But there were some surprises. For one thing, I expected that atheists were going to be among the nicest people on the planet. They could afford to be, I thought. They had the same truth I did. And I fully assumed that they would be kind—even if perhaps condescendingly so—and nice to those who were less enlightened than themselves. But this was not what I found. The atheists I was meeting were cynical, demeaning, even petty to the point of being cruel. Christians were not pitied; they were fodder for ridicule. I had felt so freed by becoming an atheist that I wanted that same epiphany for others. I couldn't understand why the atheists in my acquaintance didn't long for this same epiphany for those non-atheists they met.

If you stand for nothing, there is little one can say to challenge you.

Over time, I actually came to view atheists (still my own camp) as great cowards. While I was one of them, I grew to respect them less and less. It seemed to me that they loved taking juvenile shots at those making worldview claims, but that they wanted to do so from a vantage point that stood for nothing, giving them safety and refuge from having shots taken at their own views. If you stand for nothing, there is little one can say to challenge you. I distanced myself more and more from this group to which I belonged. I still believed I had the truth, but I had it in general isolation. Many of my friends possessed some level of faith, from being deists to full-out Christians. I quietly continued to carry my worldview, comfortable in my thinking, and went about happily living my life.

And then I had a child.

I am convinced that God often reaches out to us through our children because it is the one place where the walls of our heart are most thin, most vulnerable, most likely to be open. I shared my story with you earlier about the medical emergency that accompanied the birth of our firstborn son. That first surgery was a jolt in my previous sunshine-filled worldview.

Life wasn't going quite as planned. But this was a minor glitch, I convinced myself. We'll take care of this bump in the road, and then turn our backs on it, as though it never happened. But it turned out to be just the beginning.

A year had passed, and our son was now scheduled for a reconstructive surgery that was to be a simple, one-time event, correcting the residual medical issues from that first surgery a year before. It was supposed to be a breeze. It was supposed to be the end of this painful ordeal. It was supposed to be our new beginning. But someone clearly had not gotten that memo, because things did not go according to plan.

I believe that God sent me a gift during this difficult time, a message that would eventually open the door to my heart.

We took him home thinking we'd been given a new lease on life, only to discover that every few days or weeks we would be back in the emergency room, performing lifesaving procedures to save this increasingly sick child. Through seven weeks of uncertainty, of continued ER visits, of puzzlement from us and specialists alike, the truth was revealed. The surgery that was supposed to be our new beginning hadn't worked. So yet another surgery was performed as a stopgap measure until a new plan could be developed.

This precious child of mine would go on to need ten more

surgical procedures before he was three-and-a-half. We sought out and regularly traveled to a specialist in another state. We spent much time in one of those Ronald McDonald houses—one of the best ministries to hurting parents I've *ever* come across.

When I look back at the extraordinary levels of stress that accompanied this time period, I can only liken it to being in combat. When you see a soldier who looks like he is simply taking a walk, his eyes are actually continually scanning the landscape, constantly looking for something out of place, anything that indicates approaching trouble. He can never let his guard down. His eyes are always open a little too wide. If you ask him how he is, he'll give you a simple, polite answer. He has no time for protracted social interaction. There's too much to do. Too much at stake. He must remain vigilant, even though exhausted, even though sick himself, even though far from the life he longs to return to.

That's what having a chronically ill child felt like to me. And when our son reached three-and-a-half and our ordeal was truly and finally over, I didn't believe it— at least not for a long time. After all, I had heard *that* story before, only to learn that it wasn't going to work out as planned. I now say that it took me a good year to exhale, to finally accept that life was indeed going to return to something that resembled normal or typical.

Here's the faith component to this story. In looking back, I now believe that God sent me a gift during this difficult time, a message that would eventually open the door to my heart. Just what was that message? *Carol Barnier . . . you're not in charge of squat.*

I had marched into this situation with the belief that I was in charge of my life's outcomes. I ran the controls. I was boldly charting the path of my choice. And yet here was this precious child before me, his condition taking us all down a painful path I would never have chosen if I'd had any control at all. All sense of bravado and congratulatory ego evaporated.

I can't tell you that I recognized this message at the time. It was more a heart's early awakening than it was a turnabout of belief. But as I look back, I credit those painful days as the component that shook loose my grip on my atheist worldview and allowed me to finally, after many long years, consider the possibility of there being something bigger than myself.

The process was very slow. I first became open to "a power," which rendered me a deist for a time. I became a member of the Star Wars Church of Yoda. "He's in the rocks. He's in the trees." Then I moved forward, bit by bit, finding truth in small bites, working through those questions that had plagued me earlier, and eventually finding the elegance in answers that had been written sometimes centuries before, till I found the peace that comes—not from a return to church culture, but from falling into the arms of Jesus.

It's important to me that you know that I do not believe God *caused* damage to my son's condition in order to try to get hold of my heart. Some people are comfortable going there. I am not. God doesn't need to cause harm in order to find a path to us and provide us with a gift that might be the key to our rescue. We live in a fallen world. There is more than enough evil, sickness, pain, and suffering for God to have plenty of opportunities to use as vehicles to reach out to us. He doesn't need to fabricate them. We already give Him more than enough to work with. But I do believe that He keeps His radar up, looking for those opportunities, seeking ways to connect, longing for that reconciliation, waiting for us to throw our imperfect selves back into His arms. He knows our vulnerabilities, those places that hold the most potential for an openness to Him.

And in this mother's heart for her son, He found a way to me.

Reflect: *Were you raised as a Christian? Have you ever had doubts serious enough to cause you to leave the church? What brought you back? If you were not raised as a Christian, when did you become a believer? Spend a few moments reflecting on how you got where are today in the faith.*

Chapter 21

God,
the Artist

It had been over fifteen years since I'd stood in line to take communion, long enough for the ritual to now feel unfamiliar and awkward. I stepped out into the line, but I felt that my presence there was wrong, glaringly inappropriate. I *knew* just how far I'd fallen from God's original intentions for me. He'd had a great plan for me, and I had arrogantly squandered it. Even though I had now humbly come back to Him, it seemed presumptuous to step out into this line and think I had the right to partake of the gift of His Son along with all these other folks. I sensed that at any minute, someone would tap me on the shoulder and say, "Oh no, not you. This isn't for you. You should go stand over there and wait. We'll let you know when we're done." And what's more, I'd have said, "Deal. Got it. I understand." I was just so happy to be God's own that if those were the rules, I would have completely understood.

And yet . . . that's not God.

That's not how He operates.

I was still under some powerful misconceptions. I didn't yet have my head and heart wrapped around some of the truths of God.

The first one that was so hard for me to understand was that when it comes to God's grace through His Son . . . everyone is invited. Even I was invited. There isn't a good line and a bad line. No matter how far one might fall, when you finally turn to Him, you're in. Full fellowship. Just like the father in the Prodigal Son's own life. The calf is sacrificed. A party is given. And you are invited to participate. No second-class status.

He can astound us all with His ability to take horrid circumstances and use them to make something beautiful and new.

The other truth I hadn't yet grasped was that the unworthy were the very ones for whom communion was instituted. This "pass" that God was clearly extending on my behalf, in truth, had to be extended on everyone's behalf. We're all second-class. No one stepping into that line was worthy. Not even remotely. No one even comes close to attaining the required holiness of God that could render him worthy on his own. No one—not me, not others, not a soul—actually deserves this gift. And if God looked upon any of us with a clear eye of who we are, we would all be doomed. But instead, we are almost bizarrely fortunate that Christ has chosen to do something on our behalf. When God looks at us, when there is a direct line of sight from His eye to our heart (a line that would otherwise spell our destruction), suddenly Christ leaps into view, directly into that line of sight, asking God to look at us through the prism of His own Son. Then and only then do we have the amazing privilege of being seen well in the eyes of God.

Plan B

God indeed did have an original Plan A for me. I stepped away from it. I lost that opportunity. I decided to create my own plan and see what I could do. Then, eventually, I came back to Him and said, "Here. This is what I have. It's a mess. But it's Your mess now. I'll happily become whatever You'd like to make of this."

So He created Plan B. Now you might expect that Plan B is going to be a secondary plan, a mere shadow of the original first choice. I would have thought so too. That would have been fair, just, and right. But instead God delights in creating another first plan—a second plan just as beautiful as the first. I almost think it's fun for Him, for I've seen Him take the most ugly and unlikely experiences of my life and somehow use them as part of something good, something beautiful.

This is the same God who came up with the design of the stars, the amazing number of shades of green, the beauty of intricate patterns found in mathematics. I've long been delighted by the many patterns that reside in the number 9. These wonderful, even playful, patterns existed thousands of years before the first person ever even noticed.

This is the same God who created taste. While He could have provided us with one basic food to eat, much as He did for the panda and the anteater, He instead gave us thousands of choices, colors, textures, and combinations that not only provide nutrition, but are a feast for our palates.

He could have made just one, or five, or even a thousand types of beetles. But perhaps just to be playful, He made over 300,000 that we know of so far. Delighting in just *making* is who He is. And if He can pour so much detail and fun and amazement into things in His world, just imagine what He can do in the lives of any one of His children.

I know your children may be making some horrific decisions. The repercussions of their choices may be bringing profound pain into your world. But if these same children one day take their hearts and hand them over to the God of the universe, He can astound us all with His ability to take those same horrid circumstances and use them to make something beautiful and new.

It's what He does. It's who He is.

God is an artist. And luckily for us, *we* are His favorite medium.

—*๛*—

May God bless you with the courage and strength needed for the battles that lay ahead.

May God gift you with glimpses of your child's heart's turning that would sustain you during this difficult season of waiting.

May God bring before your child someone who is perfectly suited to influence their journey and create a longing that can only be filled in the arms of Jesus.

May you find not only an ability to survive these struggles, but to experience true joy, even now, simply because *you* are His, a condition that does not change with the state of any of the world's prodigal journeys.

May you one day see this wandering child restored to faith.

Reflect: *What are some things about God—His character, His works on our behalf, His creativity—that amaze and encourage you?*

Bonus Section

So far this book has focused its lens deep inside the family. We've talked about individual kids—their mistakes, their journeys. We've talked about parents—responses that can build bridges and responses that can cause damage. Our attention has been tightly focused on the front lines, those one-on-one interactions at the micro-level: the family.

But what about pulling the camera back and looking at a wider shot? What about the macro-response of the church body? What could the church itself be doing that would improve the odds of a child leaving the faith? What things should the church stop doing that are proving to be stumbling blocks to this generation?

It's important to be clear that this section is not addressed to parents of prodigals. These weary parents already have too much on their plate.

But for those of you in a position to have an impact on the church's current response to prodigals and their families, it's worth taking a look at possible areas that might be due for some reflection and change.

In this section, we'll also be looking at some excerpts of eye-opening interviews from prodigals who have returned. Their experiences are useful for both families and the church.

You'll also be given some resources as well as a website you can visit where the full interviews with these prodigals will be posted, as well as new responses by others who choose to participate by posting their answers to the survey questions.

For the Church

Stepping Off That Coattail Faith

The flat-bottomed tourist boat skimmed along the water at a leisurely speed. Tanks, regulators, and hoses were secured and stowed all along the front. My husband and I were enjoying a sunny vacation in Grand Cayman, and we decided to do a bit of scuba diving. Read that: He would scuba dive. I would be snorkeling on top of the water looking something like free-floating bait and gazing down with admiration at my clearly much braver husband.

This region was known for a place called Sting Ray City, a spot a mile or so offshore where the long shallow reef abruptly ends, the ocean floor steeply drops, and the massive, rolling waves suddenly begin. For years, deep-sea fishermen returning from their toil had rolled in off the large waves to park in the relative safety of this calmer reef, drop anchor, and clean their catch. Soon, stingrays began coming regularly to eat the scraps thrown overboard from the fishy leftovers. These glorious undulating sheets in the water became almost tamed by the regular feeding and

constant interactions with humans. It didn't take long for someone to figure out that it was a great diving (and profit-making)
opportunity. I was enthralled at the sight of my husband and the
other divers swimming among the school of elegant, gliding rays.
This was a once-in-a-lifetime opportunity to not only view a
marvel of nature, but actually touch it.

So why was I bobbing along on top while admiring the divers
below?

I can't dive. Or to be wholly accurate, I won't dive, at least not
until I've taken the time to obtain a much better understanding of
the equipment upon which my life so clearly depends. While the
others, who'd had the same scant basic training that I'd just had
on this short little boat trip, could gleefully leap off the back of the
boat, I simply could not. And I wasn't alone.

It was an interesting exercise to quantify the students on this
boat. These newbies seemed to fall into several categories. Some
happily followed the group, just glad to be a part. *If they're all fine
with this, then so am I. If you tell me this equipment is what keeps
me alive, I'm just fine with that. I'm glad to be along for the ride with
such fun people.*

Others listened intently, anxious to follow each and every
rule. They wouldn't ever consider questioning someone in authority. If someone with credentials of any sort tells them to do something, they're generally pretty good with following along. Folks
like this get along in the world well enough, as long as they meet
no snake oil salesmen or never receive a jubilant notification that
they've won the New Zealand lottery.

Then there's another group. My group. These folks can't coop-
erate freely or embrace any activity simply because they've been
instructed to do so. That was me in this scenario. Being asked to
fully trust my life to equipment that I did not understand was
extremely difficult. Drowning was serious business for me. And I
didn't want to just *hear* that a regulator worked and would pro-

vide me with a life-preserving mix of atmospheric gasses; I needed to know why and what and how. In other words, I needed it all to make sense. While most of these tourists happily donned the equipment and headed down, a few like-minded souls joined me on bait-patrol and stayed on the surface.

This "you-gotta-show-me" attitude is selectively applied, I will admit. I probably don't understand every scintilla of jet engine design, and yet I am a calm and almost annoyingly perky flyer. But it does, nonetheless, adequately demonstrate a not uncommon type of thinking that is sensible and not altogether bad in scuba diving or in matters of faith. There is nothing wrong with wanting things we depend on, for both our mortal life and our eternal life, to make sense.

Many young people today fit in this last category. In fact, more than ever before, kids raised in the church are craving a faith that has at its base a sensible and logical explanation. They do not want to find themselves in a group of unbelievers and unable to answer basic and reasonable questions about their faith . . . questions that are certain to come.

When I was feeling a pull away from my faith, I fell into this category. I wasn't interested in a walk on the wild side as is often assumed when a child leaves the faith. I respected authority figures, loved my parents, and enjoyed church community—quite a bit in fact. But I needed my worldview to make sense. Just as I didn't want to accept that the regulator worked merely because someone said so, I also didn't want to accept that God existed in the manner and with the characteristics I was told just because someone said so. I thought God should make sense. I certainly wanted to hear your views on God, but I also wanted to understand them and be able to logically agree with your conclusions. In other words, I wanted this faith to be my own. I wanted to stop riding on my parents' faith coattails and step out with a faith that was real to me—understandable, defensible, and sensible. It isn't arrogance or disrespectful defiance to simply want your worldview to make sense. It's a reasonable and even healthy thing for a kid to push at the edges of his faith to make sure it is solid. Asking questions should not alienate anyone.

But it often does.

As I began asking questions, I made an amazing discovery. Many of the people in my faith circle had seemingly never asked these questions. They were far more comfortable following in the paths of those who'd gone before them. In retrospect, I don't fault them for their solid faith. In many ways I actually envy them. They didn't seem to struggle with questions and trust in the same ways I did. They displayed little cognitive dissonance. I saw no furrowed brow at hearing something in one sentence that seemed to contradict something said only moments ago in another. In many ways these trusting souls had my admiration.

But on the other hand, they are typically less equipped to "give the reason for the hope that [they] have" (1 Peter 3:15). They aren't skilled in defending their faith because they never felt it needed defending. In other words, they didn't have the answers because they didn't know there were any questions. So my asking of such questions made these folks either bored, annoyed, perplexed, or to my surprise, angry, any of which served to alienate them from me and from my earnest but persistent questions. Not surprisingly, I began to grow hesitant in my efforts to seek help.

We, as Christian parents, youth leaders, and other believers in the church need to be prepared to walk alongside the kids who go through a season of faith-based tire kicking. We need not panic or proclaim them as lost. In fact, we should see it for the glorious thing that it is: someone taking Jesus seriously, wanting Him in a way that is real and personal, seeking after truth. There are answers to their questions—good answers, in fact. You can cling firmly to the truth that there simply are no questions too big to undo God. In fact, that's a laughable concept. If you exhibit a quiet panic when they ask these questions, you send a secret message that says, "Don't look too closely at God; He can't withstand scrutiny." By helping our kids find the answers, the result will be a child who becomes an adult with a faith that can stand up to examination. When the world attempts to shake them, their faith needn't fall away. Why? Because they know why they know what they know.

Why Do We Believe That?

We know that kids are going to get some things wrong. After all, there's a lot to know in the Bible. It's just plain cute when they come up with things like, *The people who followed the Lord were called the twelve decibels,* or *David was a Hebrew king skilled at playing the liar,* or *Solomon had a hundred wives and seven hundred porcupines.* It's easy to smile when the answers indicate a need for increased biblical vocabulary.

But a bigger problem comes when basic tenets of doctrine are missed—or perhaps worse, basic defense-of-the-faith knowledge. This latter component will be eagerly challenged the moment our church kids step one foot from their homes.

The awareness that our church kids need a better framework or worldview, as well as solid skills at apologetics, is now getting plenty of attention. Many of our kids (or the rest of us for that matter) are not prepared to respond to the questions and challenges they will undoubtedly hear.

- If everything has a cause, where did God come from? What was *His* cause?
- Can God do anything? And if so, can He create a rock so big that He can't lift it?
- Why would you believe in a book written thousands of years ago? The integrity must certainly be lost over time. And why not believe in the holy books of other faiths?

- Don't all sincere attempts to be good basically lead to God?
- The worst events in history have been at the hands of Christians.
- Jesus is a fictitious character. He didn't even really exist.
- There are discrepancies in your "infallible" Bible.
- How can there be evil in the world if everything is created by God?

These questions are not new, and there are some very good and even elegant responses to them. But often, our Sunday schools teach Noah and the ark, year after year after year but go no deeper. Don't get me wrong. Our kids need to know about Noah. But if you happen upon a neighbor struggling with the problem of evil, sharing the story of Noah probably won't get you very far. We are failing at meeting the challenge of the Scripture that tells us to "always be prepared to give an answer to everyone who asks you to give the reason for the hope that you have" (1 Peter 3:15). We aren't prepared. In the process, not only are we losing our neighbors, we're losing our kids.

In retrospect, I think my childhood Sunday school classes did a good job of equipping me to be a part of the Christian community. But they did little to prepare me for interacting with and influencing the non-Christian community. We need to get in there, find out what questions nonbelievers are struggling with, and then get prepared. Have an answer. Know the reasons why we believe what we believe.

What a Nice Story

In Sunday school I heard Bible stories; I learned of Jonah and the big fish, Daniel in the lions' den, Jesus walking on water. Elsewhere in the building, adults in our church were often engaged in Bible *studies*, but we kids heard Bible *stories*. I came away believing that these things I learned were all allegorical, in other words, nice, lovely stories that teach concepts but weren't about actual events. It's not much of a stretch for a kid to eventually believe that *all* of the Bible is allegorical. Indeed, I've even heard adults in the church say, "It's a beautiful book of guidelines and great thoughts. But it's not meant to be taken literally."

To be fair, some of that is true. Some of the Bible *is* allegorical. When Jesus said, "I am the vine and you are the branches . . ." He wasn't suddenly sprouting green leaves. He was speaking allegorically, representatively. The truth He shared was real, but the method by which He shared it was metaphorical. But to paint the whole Bible with that brush is to miss the equally valid (and frankly fascinating) historical record within. If the Bible were simply a lovely compilation of made-up stories, then why is the city of Damascus still on the maps? If Scriptures were meant only to entertain or provide an enlightening concept, why then does it bother with long and protracted genealogies? Why are tombs found today for the folks in these "stories" if they didn't actually exist? Why are many of the places and events and people named in the Bible also named in other ancient books outside of the Christian record?

I love the story shared by Dr. Paul Maier, a professor of ancient history and well-known lecturer on the historical evidence supporting biblical integrity. He received a letter from an irate atheist who protested that Jesus hadn't actually existed. He was tired of the perpetuation of the "Jesus myth" and was stepping up to say so. The challenger went on to say if Dr. Maier could produce one example of Jesus showing up in historical documents in any place *other* than the Bible, he would send $1,000 to the professor's favorite charity. Without skipping a beat the professor said that not only could he produce one, but easily six examples of Jesus being named by books outside of the Bible. In fact, Christ was even named by authors who were actually hostile to Christianity and its subsequent movement. They had absolutely no reason to support the story line of a supposedly fabricated character. The professor respectfully sent the man a note with this information and requested that a check for $6,000 be made out to Dr. Maier's local church.

He never did hear back from him.

We rob our children of much by failing to share with them the long history and corroborating material of the Bible. We give them only a paper-thin representation of the meat and richness of Scripture. We need to approach the Bible with reverence and awe, to be sure. But we also need to approach it as a record of events that are relevant, powerful, and in many cases, verifiable. This requires a whole different approach to teaching the Bible, starting with the very language.

No more Bible stories. More Bible studies.

Watch Out for the *Ewww* Effect

I sat in the pew of a large church that would undoubtedly qualify as "mega." I had long loved the preaching of this pastor and had listened to and learned from him for years. Honestly, I still do. But on this day, I was taken aback by what I heard. He was explaining how he was out in a public setting and had seen two women passionately kissing each other. At first he hadn't known what he was seeing, but then suddenly it hit him. When he spoke about his revelation, his revulsion burst forth. When he realized this, he shared with us that in his mind he said, "I hate you! I hate what you're doing to this country. I love you, but I hate you."

Many in the congregation undoubtedly were inwardly nodding along with his stated loathing. They were comfortable in their disgust for a clearly sinful lifestyle and its supporters, with which they had so little contact or personal experience.

But let me tell you about someone else in the congregation. I imagined a young man, maybe in his late teens, sitting somewhere in the pews. He'd been secretly struggling with his sexuality for years. His same-sex attraction was tearing him up inside, and he wasn't sure where to turn. The public schools and the media were telling him this was a wonderful thing, something to be celebrated. They welcomed him and his alternative leanings. But he wasn't buying into that. He knew he needed solid advice, biblical advice, advice that would give him a clear sense of who he was in God's sight, struggles and all. *Maybe I should talk to someone. Maybe I could get someone to help me work through this. Maybe even the pastor. Maybe . . . just maybe, I can find the courage to do this.* And then he heard those words: "I hate you! I love you, but I hate you." And the next sound you heard was that of a door closing, the door of possibility through which he might have reached out for the guidance he so desperately needed. If there was any chance he might seek help at this critical moment in time, it was gone now. I think it's highly likely that such a young man existed in that large sanctuary; in fact, probably quite a few were there. I sat there aching for those young men and young women somewhere in the seats who had just quietly died inside.

When I see a reaction like the one this pastor displayed, I've come to call it the "Ewww Effect." To be fair, it's a dynamic that has its roots in a good and even noble place, from a desire for something worthwhile. It comes cloaked in the honorable robes of a search for personal holiness . . . a legitimate and worthy desire to be set apart for Christ. No problem there. That's something we should all be striving for. But the place where we get into trouble is when we become so inwardly focused, so driven in our desire to be clean and holy, that we no longer know how to reach out and touch those whose lives are unholy. We start to develop the Ewww Effect. We come upon some sin, and we're so disgusted by it that we quickly turn away. We may find that we are so uncomfortable around sin that we no longer know how to share Christ's love with the sinner. We no longer know how to speak to the woman at the well. We no longer know what to do when the modern day equivalent of a leper comes and takes a seat beside us.

Christ certainly wasn't drawn to sin. He was never wishy-washy on the concept of right and wrong. But He was so drawn to the sinner that no one who reached out to Him would ever feel the Ewww Effect. They wouldn't feel it because it wasn't there. Touching and loving the unholy didn't in any way remove Christ's holiness. On the contrary, it fulfilled it. That's why when others were horrified that a Samaritan woman might interact with them, Jesus went up and started a conversation. That's why when a woman known as a "sinner" wrapped her hands and her hair all about Jesus' feet, He praised her for her act. When a leper came to Him begging to be healed, instead of standing at a safe distance and pronouncing him clean, Jesus reached out and grabbed hold of the man's leprous hand, healing his skin and probably his soul that very day.

Christ, as head, *our* head, is the model of how we should interact with others. The head leads. The body should follow. I've long maintained that I can tell a great deal about the heads of businesses by how their executive assistants interact with people on the phone. These first-encountered gatekeepers will frequently be the extended voice and mentality of their boss. I know that they would never employ a rude or dismissive tone, often within earshot of their bosses, if they weren't given a tacit blessing by the boss to do so. What I hear in them, I assume comes from the top. I assume I'm hearing the head when I listen to the staff.

The same dynamic can occur in churches. Much of a congregation's response to the already hurting parents of prodigals will have to come from the head down. They will be watching you and listening to you and how you feel about those who stray. They will either turn toward the wounded and sinners of the world, or they will turn away from them. They will apply disdain or compassion. They will show the face of Jesus, or they will show the face of disgust. And chances are . . . they'll be following your lead. So lead well. Lead with love. Lead with truth. Lead as Christ leads us.

A Better Look at Mom and Dad

The family is in trouble. Signs that this is so are all over. But exactly *how* it is in trouble and what should be done about it is highly debated. Some have noticed that many of the best-known atheists in history (Freud, Sartre, Nietzsche, Hume, even Madelyn Murray O'Hair) had very damaged relationships with their fathers. The conclusion therefore is that a damaged relationship with an earthly father translates into a damaged understanding of a heavenly Father.

Others decry the divorce rate. Still others the digital explosion that keeps many family members hovering over a small keyboard rather than engaged in conversation. All of these issues are worth the attention being given them.

But a less obvious and yet perhaps more insidious problem is the prevailing view in media and culture that all parents are idiots. This may seem a small complaint, but I think the ramifications are much greater than you'd suspect.

Children are expected to recognize that parents aren't to be trusted, that they are hopelessly out of touch, and that kids who want the real scoop must turn to their peers for direction and truth. Another angle on this same issue is the myth of adolescence. We are convinced that kids *must* go through a phase where they rebel, disrespect adults, and engage in risky behavior. Sometimes we witness the unfortunate example of a celebrity whose adolescent phase continues deep into adulthood. But the truth is, for thousands of years, this period of rebellion was not a thing to be expected. Certainly there were some examples of kids who did this (such as the Prodigal Son himself), but the vast majority of kids respected their elders and wanted to be like them. They enjoyed their place in the family. In fact, the family itself was the defining unit . . . not self.

This complete reversal of thousands of years of historical

precedence is such an accepted premise that it has even found its way into well-intended youth group programs. Some youth leaders convey the message *I know you can't talk to your parents . . . but you can always talk to me.* Without a doubt, they mean well. Their intentions are good. And they may even know of some difficult situations in which they are right to try to get this child to open up to another adult who can intervene for them. But the vast majority of the time this is not the case.

Start looking for this premise in the TV shows your kids watch. The main character, the kid, is the smart, clever, and competent one. The kid puts up with the parents, or more often, overtly ridicules them. And frankly, when you see these shows, it makes sense, because most of the time the parents are caricatures of parents. Befuddled, goofy, overbearing, dim. They are easy targets for ridicule. No one is standing up and saying, "No, that is not what parenting looks like."

I'm just as vulnerable. I have long loved the show *Everybody Loves Raymond* (and still get to enjoy it in reruns), and to be fair, it generally portrays wonderful family values. But I saw a different side of the program when talking to Charlie, a father at my church, who was frustrated by the image of dads that it displays. He said the idea of a father who's always taking the easy way out, not helping in the home, and generally disinterested in proactive parenting is a slap in the face to all of the dads who are purposefully engaged with their kids every day. He went on to say that he works hard to connect with his kids, to be there for all the basketball games, to have a relationship that brings security to their lives. While he could see the humor in the sitcom, he also felt our culture lumps a lot of fathers in with Raymond—fathers who don't deserve the dubious honor.

We may easily dismiss this tendency as a simple excursion into humor, but the damage may be more profound than we at first perceive. Can you imagine if two hundred years ago parents came to the door of the local one-room schoolhouse only to find someone standing outside barring them from seeing what's going on inside? "You shouldn't be spying on your kids," chastises the entry guard. Not only would that be seen as odd, it simply wouldn't have been tolerated.

Yet that was the accusation of a news reporter who was covering a new phone messaging system that was being put into place in New York City schools. In case of bad weather, a call was automatically put out to parents in a variety of languages. School closings and vacation dates were likewise put into the notification system. But here's the one that really irked this reporter. If a child has not shown up to school, the parent is notified. The reporter thought this was wrong, even frightening, and even went on to suggest that perhaps a legal remedy should be considered. Why? Because parents shouldn't *spy* on their children.

This concept of parents who can't be trusted to work for the best interest of their children is a relatively new idea in the history of family dynamics. And it has a more alarming implication. It wasn't that long ago when changes were made allowing underage girls to get abortions without parental notification. This clear breakdown in empowering parents to care and advocate for their children has created a serious challenge for those working to restore sense to the law. And mind you, in many of the same states with these laws on the books, the girls can't get their ears pierced, visit a tanning booth, or obtain a tattoo without parental consent. No, that would be inappropriate. But with a little legal paperwork, they can undergo the physically dangerous and emotionally damaging process of an abortion and a parent or legal guardian need never know of it.

While I know that there are parents who are indeed so flawed as to not be worthy of their children's respect, I believe that they are the exception, not the rule. The vast majority of parents are highly invested in the well-being of their kids. Most would gladly die for them.

It's time for a concerted effort to reverse the increasingly commonplace belief that parents are idiots, fathers are disinterested, mothers are unaware. And this assumption needs to be actively pursued and exposed by the church, even the youth group leaders. We need to make clear the damage that this popular lie produces and come back to a place where kids can access the wisdom and experience of the people who parent and love them. By and large, parents are still the best advocate for the welfare and concerns of a child. And we need to put this truth back in its place.

Whatever Happened to Sin?

Let me start by saying that I fully understand why sin has fallen out of favor. I don't mean outside of the church. Sin has never been a popular topic there. I'm talking about the lack of "sin" being discussed *inside* the church. Sermons today cover a lot of territory, but telling people about their sinful nature has all but disappeared in many churches. But I think I understand the reason why.

Let's go back to my childhood. The temperature inside the tin building was at least 90 degrees. Cardboard fans fluttered over the faces of people who had tightly crammed in their seats side by side with barely a hair's width between one another. The wooden slats of the fold-down chairs stuck to the backs of my sweating legs and left imprints when we all stood to sing. For years I mused that perhaps *this* was what was meant when it was said that God would put His mark upon you.

At the front of the crowd, on a raised platform, was an evangelist who'd been brought in for a week of camp meetings. Translation? A week of hearing all about sin. Sin in our lives. Sin in our homes. Sin in our schools. Sin in our minds. Sin that left its ugly stain on us. Sin. Sin. Sin. If you didn't know you were a sinner before, you did now. This evangelist had a rise-and-fall vocal pitch that would bellow and scream our unworthiness before God. And the solution was always the same: the altar call. The organist played music that was designed to prick the heart of those listening, calling them forward to the altar, forward to the place of confession. If you didn't come down, you could almost feel the heat of Satan's fires licking at your heels.

Maybe you remember such scenarios from your own tradition. Some problems were apparent with this approach. One was the belief that one could only turn to God via an altar call. Another was that the staging of this event could make a person feel guilty even if they were already a Christian. But the biggest flaw of this sin-screaming event was its lack of grace, which was seldom mentioned as part of the salvation package. And such an emphasis on sin almost always gives rise to its ugly offspring, legalism. Then self-righteousness. Then pride.

So the tide turned. People stepped away from the hellfire-and-brimstone message and began speaking of God's grace. Pastors now regularly preach of His forgiveness, His patience, His instruction, His heart, His wishes for our good. Sermons today showcase God's abundant grace, the amazing grace we'd missed in previous years. But . . . an imbalance in an opposite direction is still an imbalance. If this is indeed yet another skewed and lopsided message, what are the repercussions?

Every generation has had some problems with kids leaving the church. However, they typically return when they marry and begin to have kids. They may risk their own well-being, but when it comes to something as precious as their own children, they have traditionally decided it's time to get serious about the faith. But today's generation doesn't so easily fit into that mold.

When I pondered this change, I came away believing that perhaps our movement away from sin might have something to do with it.

Thirty years ago, if you had asked a young married couple, "Don't you want your children to know about Jesus? Don't you want them to be saved?" the answer would be "Yes" and that would have had an impact on their choices for their children's sakes, if not their own. But today, when our culture accepts living together before marriage, praises drive for material wealth and comfort, promotes doing what feels right, claims all truth is relative . . . when you say to parents in that mix of cultural values, "Don't you want your children to be saved?" I think that for many the answer is "Saved from what?" The thinking has shifted.

In an equally telling comparison, parents a hundred years ago would tell their children they wanted them to grow up to be good. Now the objective has changed. We say we want them to grow up to be happy. If there is a hereafter with an interested God watching over our actions, then being good matters. But if this life is it, if this is all we get, then being happy is a perfectly reasonable goal. So if adults are already basically happy, they've arrived. There is no additional moral or spiritual attainment to be desired.

What's missing in this? I think the answer might just be sin. People don't feel a compulsion to be rid of the sin in their lives if they don't first recognize that sin is there. No matter how much material gain you've accumulated, no matter how nicely you behave, your need for something to bridge the gap between you and God doesn't change.

I humbly suggest that sin needs to reenter the church lexicon, that we need to make clear to people their inability to attain goodness without God. We need a clearer sense of just what *good* is, for our current watered-down, weak-tea version is being offered up for public consumption as adequate, acceptable, all that there is. The greatness and holiness of God and *His* version of goodness needs to be reintroduced, including our bumbling and impossible efforts to attain it. We do our listeners no favors by leaving this out. It creates a false sense of security. But I implore you to couple it heartily with the grace that God the Father Himself always does. Grace without sin is sweet-tasting candy. All sugar. No nutrition. Sin without grace is bad-tasting medicine. All pain. Likely to be spit out. No healing.

Dismantling the Club

Church is this wonderful place for fellowship and connection. A gathering of like-minded individuals has its own rewards. We feel a part of something, a family of sorts, a place where we belong. It's a community where people will rally to one another's needs, lift one another up in prayer, and love one another. All of this is a good thing and should be encouraged. But it's oh-so-easy to slip from good fellowship into club membership. Many congregants lose their way, forget the charter of the church as a hospital for the sick and a lighthouse for the lost, and begin to believe it's their own personal gated community. A statement by Leonard Ravenhill grabs this thought well: "The church used to be a lifeboat rescuing the perishing. Now she's a cruise ship recruiting the promising."

My mother always said that a church without children is a dying church. She and my pastor father regularly drove our noisy, battered, orange VW van around town early on Sunday mornings, gathering up any children in our little community whose parents would part with them for a few hours. Sometimes the parents had a sincere desire for their children to go to church. But honestly, just as often the parents were a little hungover and were frankly glad to have the kids and their noise out of the house for a few hours. Sometimes the parent was a single mom struggling with depression, and she was glad to give her child the advantage of being out of the gloom of her home for a while. Sometimes we would walk into houses where the sadness or tension was thick in the air. The situations were often horrible. Out of such circumstances, my parents would round up various kids from the area and bring them to church. They'd plop 'em down up front where they could keep an eye on 'em, where, not surprisingly, these kids would proceed to wiggle, misbehave, and talk when they shouldn't. In other words . . . they didn't know church culture. They didn't know how to behave. This was all new to them. There was a lot they didn't get right. But they did get to hear the amazing news that somewhere in the universe was this God . . . who thought they were precious.

And unique.

And had a plan for them. Man . . . that was news.

Once, when this busload of kids was showing their lack of church culture etiquette, one church member bitterly complained to my mother. "Those children are dirty and misbehaved. They're sitting up there on the front pew, and they have no idea how they're supposed to act in church. What are you going to do about it?"

My mother's answer? My dear mother, who was very uncomfortable with confrontations? She took a breath and said, "You mean, what am I going to do with a bunch of children who are so new to church that they don't even know how to behave?" Another big breath. "I'm going to go out and get as many more of them as I can."

What's the mentality in your church? Do people have a clear sense that it is Christ's place, His hospital, where the sick come to be made whole? Or is it their clubhouse, where they gather together to enjoy people like themselves, feeling comfortable in their camaraderie, and partaking of all the perks and status this membership offers?

What would happen if your church actively began to pray that God would send to you those no one else wanted? The marginalized. The dismissed. The mocked. That's exactly what happened in Pastor Doug's church. And he'll be the first to warn you, "Watch what you ask for."

Pastor Doug (Doug's and Brandon's names have been changed

for privacy) had a heart for the spiritually broken. He communicated this love for the lost through his sermons and his own witness. As a result, his congregation soon joined him in his heart's mission. They began to pray that God would send them broken people, needy people, people "nobody else wanted." And one day, in a clear answer to those prayers, in walked Brandon. Brandon had already been asked to leave two churches. His presence was disruptive. His situation too much for local church members' sensibilities to endure. And what was the problem with Brandon? He was a cross-dresser on his way to becoming a transsexual. He came with a flawed self-image that convinced him he was supposed to have been a woman. He firmly believed he had been born with a profound birth defect: the body of a man.

Brandon immediately sought out Pastor Doug personally, to ask him if he would be permitted to attend this church. Why? Because in the last church, the pastor had *said* he was welcome, but after Brandon stayed following the service for the church's coffee hour, he received a phone call that told him he'd crossed the line. He was now informed by the pastor that he could continue to attend, but he must sit in the back where others couldn't see him, and he must never, under any circumstances, get involved in church fellowship activities.

Come, but then go. Those were the rules.

So when Brandon visited this new church and approached Pastor Doug, he was ready to hear anything. He was also ready to make this his last effort at trying to connect with a church and a faith community. If this didn't work, it was over. He'd give up on churches and on God. He had made this determination in his heart before even stepping through the door. But God had sent him to the right place, a place where people had been actively praying that someone just like him might come. Pastor Doug made a fateful decision. *Yes. You may come. In fact, you are welcome.*

Now was Pastor Doug totally comfortable with this? Yes and no.

This was new territory. There wasn't a denominational handbook on how to assimilate cross-dressers into the Christian community. But he was comfortable that Brandon was a direct answer to their prayers and that this was the best place for Brandon to be; a wounded man in a hospital for the wounded. And so they proceeded.

Not surprisingly, people complained. They wanted him out. This was unseemly. This was uncomfortable. This was not what church was supposed to look like. And how on earth do we explain him to the children? But the pastor stuck to his guns, and as a result, many people left. But those who remained were committed to those original prayers—*send us those no one else wants.* They prayed with Brandon. They worshiped with Brandon. They ate with Brandon. They incorporated him so completely into their body of fellow seekers that the women's Bible study group invited him to join them. *And it was here*, surrounded by a group of women, that it eventually became very clear to Brandon that he was not meant to be a woman. The humor of this occurrence is not lost on me. Indeed, perhaps the best way to dissuade any male of their inclination to be a woman is to let them spend some exclusive time in our uniquely feminine community. Nonetheless, it was here that Brandon realized that he was created by design, with intent, for a purpose. He dug into Scripture, found the truth of God's plan for him, discovered his preciousness in God's sight as a man. He acquired a new awareness of the lies that had been told to him about his sexuality from the time he was a very young child. He found clarity and a new confidence in who he was in Christ. And his days as a woman were over.

Brandon was given time to walk in the light that he currently had. It was not an instantaneous event. As long as he was actively seeking God's direction for his life, he was given the same margin for seeking Christ as the rest of us. When you ask Pastor Doug today about those difficult years, he will tell you he's sorry that so many people left. Not because their feelings were hurt. Not because they were right. And not because he felt the loss of their contribution to the church community. But because they missed out on God's miracle in this man's life. They missed out on the power of prayer. And they missed out on the importance of radical obedience to the concept of this being *God's* church and not their own.

This is one of the toughest situations I can currently imagine. This issue is so very sensitive that people often cannot even hear a different perspective without leaping to a belief that it is accompanied by a softness on sin. I believe that to be an unfortunate and false leap. But I still suspect that there isn't a church out there that would not struggle with this one.

The reason I share it here is because it provides a powerful illustration of the line between fellowship and membership. This club mentality, albeit usually in a less dramatic sense, still has an impact on prodigals. They feel the unspoken club rules. They sense the social contract that is expected and fulfilled by the contented members. And they know that if they break one of these "rules," they will be out. Ranks will close. Church culture will triumph.

Creating fellowship is not a bad objective. And I understand that there is a difficult dance involved in reconciling the two objectives of enjoying each other in Christ and fulfilling the biblical mandate of reaching the lost. But these two objectives are not on par with each other. They are not equal. And if ever there comes a time when they are in conflict, the next action is very clear. Dr. Joe McKeever, longtime pastor and more recently director of missions for over a hundred New Orleans churches, states it well.

According to Matthew 16:18, it's Jesus' church.
According to Acts 20:28, it's God's.
Same difference.
Pastor, I know your name is on the sign out front. Thank you for your faithful work, but it's not your church.

Deacons, Thank you for your years of sacrificial effort and service. But it's not your church.

Church members with seniority, Thank you for hanging in there through good times and bad, but it's not your church.

Those who have given the most money, Thank you for your generosity and sacrifices, but it's not your church.

And church polity aside, congregation, Thank you for coming and working and giving and praying, but it's not your church.

It's His Church. And the only question on our lips every time we meet to do His business should be "What would You have us do?"

The difficulty here is not lost on me. I love my fellow brothers and sisters in Christ. I enjoy the time in their company and corporate worship. I love how I can turn to them for emotional and spiritual support. I love that when there is a medical crisis or great individual need in this body of believers, they will rally and care and pray for one another like no other people. I fully understand the natural inclination to protect this social dynamic as it has sustained me and others more than once.

But we must not grow so comfortable in the trenches that we lose sight of the battle that put us in the trenches in the first place. God gave us a task to do, to be the face of Jesus to an unbelieving world. And in His goodness, He made the difficult task almost enjoyable by giving us the warmth of this amazing family of fellow believers who are also given this task. But we must never forget that this fellowship, while wonderful to be a part of, is merely a perk of being in the body of Christ; it is not the objective.

May God's hand of blessing be on you and all those in leadership around you as you work to make Christ known to an unbelieving and unknowing world.

May God give you great courage to stand up for His will, His heart, and His wishes at times when it is more comfortable to do otherwise.

May you be given the gift of seeing your work bear fruit, growing people in closer relationship to Christ.

May you not tire but be blessed with encouragers, your own Barnabas team, to lift you up and remind you of your worth.

May you find joy erupting in your life, again and again, to renew you for your labors.

And may God saturate you with peace of knowing that no matter how difficult the road, you are His, and He is yours.

What Some Other Prodigals Have to Say

Wouldn't you love to read the thoughts of some other prodigals? What do they wish their families had done differently? What changes might have influenced their desire to walk away from God? What did it take to bring them back? Prodigals have so many different paths away from faith. And yet, they surprisingly have many things in common.

I decided to interview several prodigals. I posed the same ten questions to each of them. Their backgrounds and situations are quite varied. Some are housewives. Some are pastors. Some are writing from prison. And some are still struggling to reconnect clearly with their Creator in a way that makes sense of their world. Among the answers given, you may find something that sounds like your child and gives you a sense of understanding that you perhaps missed before.

Below you'll find a few selected answers to some of the questions. But if you'd like to look at any individual's full set of responses, check out our website at prodigalplace.com.

Question 1: *What are some things your family did well in responding to your departure from their faith?*

For the majority of the time that I drifted from the Lord, I was in the US Navy and stationed overseas in Japan. Consequently, I had no daily contact with my family and very little other contact, with the exception of the occasional phone call and weekly letters. My father was (and is) a pastor, and at the end of every letter he wrote me every week, he would close with the phrase *Remember who you are and whose you are.* I knew what he meant. In his way, he was admonishing me to remember that I was his and my mother's son. But even more, he wanted me to recall the fact that I had placed my faith in Christ at a very young age, and as a result, I belonged to Christ. That not-so-subtle reminder was not lost on me, even though I continued to live a very riotous life. (**Craig D.**)

Question 2: *What are some things your family could have done better in responding to your change of faith?*

I believe that I was judged a bit too harshly. Yes, they did well by not pushing, but at the same time I felt like the mistakes I was choosing to make were irreversible. And that if my family was giving up on me, then I felt that God was too. (**Marianne O.**)

Question 3: *Can you share an example of how the church (pastors, teachers, youth leaders, fellow Christians) responded well during the time you were leaving the faith?*

As far as I can remember they did not respond positively or negatively because they did not respond at all. I think I just fell through the cracks. However, the memories of my youth group years (functions, camps, etc.) are sweet, and I will always treasure them as they contributed to showing me the love of God at an early age. I do not think many churches invest in their children like they should. These are the future generations of our faith—and we should not just entertain but train each one specifically in the way he or she should go. Like I said, my memories are sweet, but there was no investment in me.

Closing the gap between the elders and the future generations would benefit all. (**Nathan S.**)

Question 4: *Are there ways that the church or those in the church responded badly or could have responded better to your departure from faith?*
I wish I could have formulated and asked the questions that I wrestled with as a teen. Providing a forum for kids to ask questions may have saved me from leaving the faith. (**Heather M.**)

Question 5: *In the responses of Christians, what surprised you most?*
That they were so easily able to judge me for my choices, and that I was, for lack of a better word, expendable to them. (**Marianne O.**)

Question 6: *Was there a particular event that had an impact on your leaving the faith?*
I was in school to be a minister. I got a phone call one night after 9 p.m. from my mother, stating that my father had been diagnosed with brain cancer. I remember feeling very betrayed. In my mind the question began: how could a God who I had surrendered my whole life to, allow my father to get cancer? (**Jeff J.**)

Question 7: *Was there a particular event that had a positive impact on your return to faith?*
Spending a couple weeks in L.A. (on assignment for a magazine in New York), I spent some time with my aunt. Aunt Mary looked just like my mom and had a voice that was just like my mom's, but she was active in the Wiccan faith, and that startled me (that she believed so differently from my mom). I was torn between my evangelical Christian upbringing and the girl I had been dating

(who claimed to be a Zen Buddhist) and the girl I was spending time with in L.A. (who was a practicing Catholic), and that caused me to find a Bible, drop it open, and ask God to reveal the truth to me. The passage that I opened to was Psalm 51, which is a psalm of repentance that immediately hit home the reality of my situation. I broke down crying, asking for mercy from God. (**Jeff S.**)

(Carol adds, "I particularly love Jeff's answer here because it so beautifully displays God's knowledge in just who should be brought into the path of our prodigal to have the most impact. Not one of us would probably have prayed, 'Oh Lord, please bring an active Wiccan into the path of my son.' And yet it was exactly what he needed to reassess and reevaluate what he believed.")

Question 8: *Since God is willing to make something good of any and all things, have you felt, in looking back, that some good thing has emerged from the prodigal journey that you took?*

Absolutely. I can talk to people who are rebelling or are struggling with whether or not God will forgive them for what they have done, and I can talk to them as one who knows the pains and hurt they are dealing with. Furthermore, as a pastor who has experienced what I have, I believe it makes me more accessible to prodigals who need someone to talk to and be real with . . . someone who won't be pious and judgmental, but will still call them to repentance and reconciliation. My experiences have also allowed me to be very application-driven in my sermons. Oftentimes I use scenarios in which the point of my sermon can be applied, and these scenarios come directly from my own experiences. (**Craig D.**)

Question 9: *If you were able to step back in time and chat with yourself before you stepped away from your faith, what might you say to yourself?*

The main thing that I would say to myself is that Christians are human beings, which means that we're fallible, not perfect. The things we do, as much as they're intended to be Christ-honoring, aren't always. The most important thing isn't to focus on other people's behavior or other people's relationships with one another. The most important thing is to focus on my own relationship with God and to let God take care of the rest. I was never designed to be the judge. I was never designed to be the jury. That's His role, not mine. I've got enough flaws and I've done enough things wrong myself that I simply need to focus on my relationship with Him. He'll take care of everything else. (**Tara A.**)

Question 10: *How would you advise parents of a prodigal today?*
The best advice I can give is don't push too hard, but at the same time, show your children that though they may make decisions that will affect their lives, they will never do anything to fall out of your love or God's grace. Sometimes we may be stubborn and have to learn the hard way . . . but as long as we know you love us, we will eventually come back. The fear of being judged as a failure or not good enough is a powerful force that keeps most kids away. Whether we act like it or not, we need the reassurance that we are loved, accepted, cherished, and above all, good enough, no matter what. (**Marianne O.**)

For the full interview from each prodigal—or to comment or share your own story—go to prodigalplace.com. My prayer is for an opportunity for healing on both sides: answers for parents who want to understand, and sharing for prodigals who want to be understood.

More Resources

Especially for parents:
Gen Ex-Christian: Why Young Adults Are Leaving the Faith ... And How to Bring Them Back, Drew Dykes
How to Really Love Your Adult Child, Gary Chapman, PhD and Ross Campbell, MD
Prodigals and Those Who Love Them, Ruth Bell Graham
Praying for Your Prodigal Daughter, Janet Thompson
Praying Prodigals Home, Quin Sherrer

For those who question or would like a better understanding of the Christian faith:
Coffee House Chronicles (a series of three short books), Josh McDowell and Dave Sterrett
- *Is The Bible True ... Really? A Dialogue on Skepticism, Evidence, and Truth*
- *Who Is Jesus ... Really? A Dialogue on God, Man, and Grace*
- *Did the Resurrection Happen ... Really? A Dialogue on Life, Death, and Hope*

Not God's Type: A Rational Academic Finds a Radical Faith, Holly
   Ordway
*The Case for Christ: A Journalist's Personal Investigation of the
   Evidence for Jesus,* Lee Strobel
Walking from East to West, Ravi Zacharius
I Don't Have Enough Faith to Be an Atheist, Norman L. Geisler
New Evidence That Demands a Verdict, Josh McDowell
What's So Great about Christianity, Dinesh D'Souza
Under the Influence: How Christianity Changed the World, Alvin J.
   Schmidt
The Reason for God: Belief in an Age of Skepticism, Timothy Keller
Mere Christianity, C. S. Lewis
*Why Trust Jesus?: An Honest Look at Doubts, Plans, Hurts, Desires,
   Fears, Questions, and Pleasures,* Dave Sterrett
*Letters from a Skeptic: A Son Wrestles with His Father's Questions
   about Christianity,* Gregory Boyd and Edward Boyd
Jesus: Legend or Lord? (audio cassette and DVD), Dr. Paul Maier
Know Why You Believe, Paul E. Little and James R. Nyquist
The Making of an Atheist, James S. Speigel

Internet:
Celebrate Recovery: www.celebraterecovery.com. Celebrate Recovery is a program designed to help those struggling with hurts,
   hang-ups, and habits by showing them the loving power of
   Jesus Christ through the recovery process. Over 700,000
   people have gone through Celebrate Recovery's program.
www.seanmcdowell.org: Check out Worldview, the speaking,
   teaching, and writing ministry of Sean McDowell. Sean's passion is to help create a paradigm shift in how we teach truth
   to the younger generation.
www.ParentsofProdigals.com: A site filled with hope, encouragement, and resources
Free online four-week Bible study on Fighting for Your Prodigal
   Child: http://biblestudies.stores.yahoo.net/fiforyoprch.html

Helpful Scripture

Psalm 16:7
Psalm 18:6
Psalm 27:13–14
Psalm 37:4
Psalm 40:1–3
Psalm 42:5
Psalm 139
Isaiah 40:28–31
Matthew 7:7
Luke 15:1–10; 18:1
Acts 17:27
Romans 8:28
Romans 8:37–39
Philippians 1:6
Philippians 4:4–7
Ephesians 3:17–21
Ephesians 6:18
Hebrews 13:5–6
James 1:2–5

Acknowledgments

The Moody Team—From the first contact through every aspect of publication, I have been blessed by the people at Moody and their gracious handling of all they do. In particular I appreciated Pam Pugh's ability to make editing fun, as well as Keith Wiederwax and his marketing skills. Most especially, I enjoyed working with Dave DeWit in shaping the various thought directions in this book. Everything he asked of me resulted in a better book.

My Thought Team—To the many people who have graciously allowed me to borrow their brains and bounce ideas off them. My pastor Paul Astbury, my first spiritual mentor Pr. Dave, and those first tier listeners, Lois Etienne and Sue McGill, who always hear of my ideas early, when they are mere nubs of thought.

My Family—My husband and children, who endure many meals of leftovers while I'm to be found on the computer, and do so with much graciousness. I simply couldn't do this without you all and your support. I especially need to thank my daughter, Katie, who is always my first reader, finest editor, and best critic since about the time she learned her ABCs.

Prodigals Everywhere—I want to thank the many prodigals who shared freely of their own journeys with me. I know it was hard sometimes, and your courage is noted. I also appreciate Shelly Esser, Paul Schwarz, and John Stonestreet, and the many others who assisted me in connecting with other prodigals.

YWAM friends—Tom, Warren, and Jim—who believed in my words long before I even knew what "platform" was. They are the reason I learned I had more than one book in me.

GENERATION EX-CHRISTIAN

GENERATION
EX-
CHRISTIAN

WHY YOUNG ADULTS ARE LEAVING
THE FAITH...
AND HOW TO BRING THEM BACK

DREW DYCK

978-0-8024-3355-7

also available as an eBook

This book will equip and inspire parents, church leaders, and everyday Christians to reawaken the prodigal's desire for God and set him or her back on the road to a dynamic faith. The book will identify seven different kinds of leavers and offer practical advice for how to connect with each type.

MOODY
PUBLISHERS